D1324778

THE
TOP 100
CHEAP EATS

THE
TOP 100
CHEAP EATS

100 DELICIOUS BUDGET RECIPES FOR THE WHOLE FAMILY

Hilaire Walden

DUNCAN BAIRD PUBLISHERS

LONDON

The Top 100 Cheap Eats
Hilaire Walden

First published in the United Kingdom and Ireland in 2010 by
Duncan Baird Publishers Ltd
Sixth Floor, Castle House
75–76 Wells Street
London W1T 3QH

Conceived, created and designed by Duncan Baird Publishers

Managing Editor: Grace Cheetham
Editor: Alison Bolus
Managing Designer: Suzanne Tuhrim
Commissioned photography: William Lingwood, Simon Smith
  and Toby Scott
Food Stylists: Sunil Vijayakar, Joss Herd and
  Marie-Ange La-Pierre
Prop Stylists: Tessa Evelegh and Helen Trent

British Library Cataloguing-in-Publication Data:
A CIP record for this book is available from the British Library

ISBN: 978-1-84483-895-0

10 9 8 7 6 5 4 3 2 1

Typeset in News Gothic
Colour reproduction by Colourscan, Singapore
Printed in Malaysia for Imago

Publisher's Note

While every care has been taken in compiling the recipes for
this book, Duncan Baird Publishers, or any other persons
who have been involved in working on this publication,
cannot accept responsibility for any errors or omissions,
inadvertent or not, that may be found in the recipes or text,
nor for any problems that may arise as a result of preparing
one of these recipes. If you are pregnant or breastfeeding or
have any special dietary requirements or medical conditions,
it is advisable to consult a medical professional before
following any of the recipes contained in this book.

Notes on the Recipes

Unless otherwise stated:
Use medium eggs, fruit and vegetables
Use fresh ingredients, and fresh herbs
Do not mix metric and imperial measurements
1 tsp = 5ml   1 tbsp = 15ml   1 cup = 250ml
• Some of the recipes in this book may contain raw or lightly
cooked eggs – these recipes are not recommended for babies
and young children, pregnant women, the elderly and those
convalescing.

CONTENTS

INTRODUCTION

Eating cheaply doesn't have to mean eating poorly, unimaginatively and boringly. Cheap food can be just as nutritious, interesting and delicious as more expensive food, which I hope this book will prove.

There are many things that you can do to cut down on food costs. For example, buy basic store-cupboard items such as pasta, rice and dried beans in large packets. Look for special offers including perishable foods that are being sold off at a reduced price because they are near their "sell by" date. Think before you throw out any food – often leftovers can be made into another meal. Look out for reduced items such as canned tomatoes and beans: any damaged can that is sold is safe to buy, but it is best to use the contents quite soon.

Try to find a market or farm shop and and discover the benefits to buying and eating seasonally. Try your hand at growing your own herbs and some vegetables too, even if you don't have much of a garden, or any garden at all.

Pots of herbs can easily be grown on sunny windowsills, and some tomatoes and beans can be grown in grow-bags and even hanging baskets.

The cost of the food is not the only contributing factor in eating cheaply: the costs of preparation and cooking also play a part. Unless you cook using gas, pans with dead-flat bottoms that sit snugly on the hob will be the most economical to use. Tight-fitting lids will also save money, as will using the most appropriate size of pan for the amount you are cooking. If you don't have a small enough pan, use dividers so you can cook two vegetables at the same time. Another way of doubling up is to steam one vegetable in a covered basket over the pan. Instead of boiling vegetables, use just a little water, and perhaps a knob of butter, and keep the lid jammed tightly on the pan, so the vegetables semi-steam. This is not only economical on fuel but also preserves more nutrients.

Above all buy sensibly, giving some thought to how or when you are going to use the purchase. If you write a menu for the week and just buy what you need, you'll find you save a lot of wastage – and money!

Chapter 1

STARTERS

There are many dishes that you can make for a first course without adding much to the overall cost of the meal. Soups are a prime example, such as Chicken & Pearl Barley Soup (see page 10). Soups have the extra plus of filling people up, especially if served with plenty of bread. In fact, serving bread with just about any first course is a useful way to reduce people's appetites by a reasonable amount at a modest cost.

It is a good idea to make use of foods when they are particularly plentiful, such as courgettes, tomatoes and lettuces in the summer. Another way to save money is to buy pieces of chicken with the bones in and simply remove any bones if necessary. Or use chicken wings that you have removed from an uncooked whole chicken – with a few extra ingredients you can make these into delicious dishes.

Marinated Halloumi Salad (see page 21)

001 Chicken & Pearl Barley Soup

PREPARATION TIME 10 minutes   **COOKING TIME** 50–60 minutes   **SERVES** 4

4–6 skinless, boneless chicken thighs
1 rosemary sprig
2 bay leaves
5 garlic cloves
200ml/7fl oz/scant 1 cup medium-bodied
   dry white wine
825ml/28 fl oz/3½ cups chicken stock
1 onion, finely chopped

1 carrot, diced
olive oil, for frying
50g/2oz/¼ cup pearl barley
½ iceberg lettuce, shredded
2 tbsp flat-leaf parsley, chopped
salt and freshly ground black pepper
freshly grated Parmesan cheese, to serve

1 Put the chicken, rosemary, bay leaves, 4 of the garlic cloves, wine and stock into a saucepan. Slowly bring just to the boil, then reduce the heat and simmer gently for 10–15 minutes, depending on size, until the chicken is just cooked through. Transfer the chicken to a plate using a slotted spoon. Reserve the stock.

2 Chop the reserved garlic clove. Fry the onion, carrot and chopped garlic in a little oil in a saucepan over a moderate heat until softened. Strain in the stock and bring to the boil, then add the pearl barley. Stir and cook for about 35–40 minutes until the barley is tender.

3 Meanwhile, chop the chicken quite finely. Add to the soup with the lettuce and parsley, when the barley is cooked. Heat gently until the lettuce has wilted. Season. Serve sprinkled with Parmesan.

002 Chickpea, Pasta & Sage Soup

PREPARATION TIME 10 minutes   COOKING TIME 25 minutes   SERVES 4

1 celery stick, chopped

1 leek, chopped

1 carrot, finely chopped

olive oil, for frying

3 garlic cloves, finely chopped

8 small sage leaves, finely chopped

400g/14oz tinned chickpeas,
   drained and rinsed

400g/14oz/1⅔ cups tinned chopped
   tomatoes

825ml/28 fl oz/3½ cups vegetable stock

100g/3½oz small pasta shapes for soup

salt and freshly ground black pepper

freshly grated Parmesan cheese, to serve

1 Fry the celery, leek and carrot in a little oil in a saucepan over a moderate heat until lightly browned. Add the garlic and sage and fry for 1 minute, then add the chickpeas, tomatoes and stock. Bring to the boil, then reduce the heat and simmer for 15–20 minutes.

2 Meanwhile, cook the pasta in a large saucepan of boiling water following the packet instructions until just cooked or al dente and drain well.

3 Pour most of the soup into a blender or food processor and reduce to a thick, chunky purée. Return to the pan, add the pasta and heat through, adjusting the thickness, if necessary, by boiling so that excess liquid evaporates, or adding more stock if too thick. Season to taste. Serve with the Parmesan.

003 Vegetable & Borlotti Soup

PREPARATION TIME 10 minutes   COOKING TIME 45 minutes   SERVES 6

1 onion, chopped
1 small leek, thinly sliced
2 celery sticks, chopped
3 garlic cloves, chopped
3–4 thyme sprigs
olive oil, for frying
1.2 litres/40 fl oz/4¾ cups vegetable stock
400g/14oz tinned borlotti beans,
    drained and rinsed

1 courgette, diced
5 tomatoes, chopped
175g/6oz frozen French beans, halved
175g/6oz/heaped 1 cup frozen broad beans
leaves from a small bunch of flat-leaf
    parsley, chopped
salt and freshly ground black pepper
6 tbsp homemade or bought pesto and
    some shaved pecorino cheese, to serve

1 Fry the onion, leek, celery, garlic and thyme in a little olive oil in a large saucepan over
a moderate heat until softened but not coloured. Add the stock and bring to the boil, then
reduce the heat, cover and simmer for 30 minutes.

2 Add the borlotti beans, courgette, tomatoes and French and broad beans and return to the boil.
Simmer for a further 10 minutes, then add the parsley, stir well and season to taste.

3 Discard the thyme and serve with pesto swirled in and scattered with some pecorino shavings.

004 Chicken Satay

PREPARATION TIME 15 minutes, plus 1–8 hours marinating **COOKING TIME** 20–25 minutes **SERVES** 4

675g/1lb 8oz boneless chicken thighs,
    cut into 2.5 cm/1in-wide strips
squeeze of lemon juice
1 garlic clove, chopped
2 tsp ground coriander
2 tsp ground cumin
1 tsp turmeric
1 tbsp dark soft brown sugar
4 tbsp coconut milk
lemon or lime wedges, to serve

SATAY SAUCE
75g/2½oz/½ cup unsalted peanuts
1 garlic clove, chopped
2 tbsp red Thai curry paste
400ml/14fl oz/1⅔ cups coconut milk
2 tbsp dark soft brown sugar
squeeze of lemon juice
dash of Tabasco sauce

1 Put the chicken into a shallow, non-metallic dish. Sprinkle with the lemon juice.

2 Combine the garlic with the spices, sugar and coconut milk to make a fairly stiff paste. Rub evenly into the meat. Cover and leave in a cool place for at least 1 hour, preferably 8 hours (in which case put it in the fridge, then remove ½ –1 hour before cooking).

3 Preheat the grill to high. Meanwhile, make the sauce by toasting the peanuts in a baking tin under the preheated grill, stirring frequently to ensure they brown evenly. Transfer to a blender or food processor. Add the garlic, curry paste and a little of the coconut milk. Mix until smooth, then add the remaining ingredients and mix until evenly blended. Pour into a saucepan. Boil for 2 minutes, then lower the heat and simmer for 10 minutes, stirring occasionally. If the sauce thickens too much, add a little water.

4 Thread the chicken on to skewers (soaked if wooden). Cook on an oiled grill rack under the preheated grill for 5–10 minutes until the chicken is cooked through.

5 Warm the sauce through, thinning if necessary with a little water, then pour into a warm jug. Serve the satays with lemon or lime wedges and the sauce.

005 Chicken Yakitori

PREPARATION TIME 10 minutes **COOKING TIME** 13–15 minutes **SERVES** 6

6 boneless chicken thighs, cut into
  2.5-cm/ 1-in pieces
12 slim leeks, outer leaves removed,
  cut into 2.5-cm/1-in lengths, or 12 fat
  spring onions, green parts trimmed and
  cut inti 2.5-cm/1-in lengths

YAKITORI DIPPING SAUCE
175ml/6fl oz/⅔ cup dark soy sauce
6 tbsp saké
6 tbsp chicken stock
50ml/1½fl oz/scant ¼ cup mirin
1 small garlic clove, finely chopped
4½ tsp caster sugar
freshly ground black pepper

1 Preheat the grill to high. Make the sauce by heating the ingredients in a saucepan over a
  moderate heat, stirring until the sugar has dissolved. Bring to the boil, then reduce the heat
  and simmer for 1 minute. Remove from the heat and leave to cool, then strain.
2 Thread the chicken, skin-side out, and the leeks or spring onions alternately on to skewers
  (soaked if wooden).
3 Pour about a quarter of the sauce into a small bowl.
4 Cook the skewers on an oiled grill rack under the preheated grill for 2 minutes, brush with the
  remaining sauce and continue cooking for 6–8 minutes, basting with the sauce frequently and
  turning once. Serve the skewers with the dipping sauce.

006 Chicken & Rice Noodle Salad

PREPARATION TIME 10 minutes, plus 1 hour marinating   **COOKING TIME** 4–5 minutes   **SERVES** 6

225g/8oz frozen skinless chicken breasts,
   thawed, cut into strips
225g/8oz rice vermicelli noodles
1 small courgette, cut into thin strips
3 tbsp coriander leaves, coarsely torn

MARINADE
1 garlic clove, crushed
1 tbsp Thai fish sauce
1 tsp Thai red curry paste
1 tsp sesame oil
1 tsp clear honey

DRESSING
3 tbsp groundnut oil
3 tbsp lime juice
4½ tsp Thai fish sauce
few drops of Tabasco sauce
2–3 tsp caster sugar

1 Put the chicken strips in a non-metallic bowl. Make the marinade by combining the ingredients. Stir into the chicken, cover and leave in a cool place for 1 hour, stirring occasionally.

2 Meanwhile, pour boiling water over the noodles and leave to soak for 4–5 minutes or according to the noodle packet instructions. Drain well and tip into a large bowl. Add the courgette and coriander.

3 Make the dressing by combining the ingredients. Pour half over the noodles, toss and then marinate in the fridge for 1 hour. Preheat the grill to high.

4 Lift the chicken from the marinade and cook on an oiled grill rack under the preheated grill for about 2 minutes on each side.

5 Divide the noodles among four bowls. Pile the chicken on top of the noodles and trickle over the remaining dressing.

007 **Lime & Honey-Glazed Chicken Wings**

PREPARATION TIME 5 minutes, plus 4–8 hours marinating   **COOKING TIME** 25–30 minutes   **SERVES** 4

12 large chicken wings, tips cut off

lime wedges, to serve

MARINADE

6 tbsp lime juice

3 tbsp honey

2 tbsp olive oil

2 tbsp dry white wine

2 tsp marjoram leaves, chopped

1 tsp thyme leaves

freshly ground black pepper

1 Place the chicken wings in a shallow non-metallic dish.

2 Make the marinade by mixing all the ingredients together. Pour evenly over the wings, turn them over to ensure they are evenly coated, then cover and leave to marinate in the fridge for 4–8 hours, turning occasionally. Remove them from the fridge ½–1 hour before cooking.

3 Preheat the oven to 200°C/400°F/Gas 6 or preheat the grill. Put the wings on a baking tray and pour any remaining marinade over the top.

4 Bake in the preheated oven for 25–30 minutes or grill for about 10 minutes on each side. Remove from the oven or grill and serve with lime wedges.

008 Herbed Fish Burgers

PREPARATION TIME 15 minutes   COOKING TIME 8–10 minutes   SERVES 6

350g/12oz white fish fillets, skinned
1–2 tbsp lemon juice
1 tbsp Worcestershire sauce
1 tsp creamed horseradish
115ml/3¾fl oz/scant ½ cup milk
1 tbsp snipped chives
1 tbsp chopped parsley

350g/12oz cooked potatoes,
  peeled and mashed with a little butter
50g/2oz/⅔ cup fresh breadcrumbs
olive oil, for frying
mixed salad leaves, to serve
mayonnaise, to serve

1 Put the fish, lemon juice, Worcestershire sauce, horseradish sauce and milk in a food processor or blender and mix until smooth. Transfer to a bowl and mix in the herbs and mashed potatoes until evenly combined.

2 Shape into 6 small burgers. Spread the breadcrumbs on a plate and coat the burgers evenly in the crumbs.

3 Heat a large non-stick frying pan and add the oil. Fry the burgers for 4–5 minutes until golden, then turn them over with a fish slice and fry on the other side for a further 4–5 minutes. Remove with the fish slice and drain on some kitchen paper.

4 Serve the fish burgers with the salad leaves and some mayonnaise for dipping.

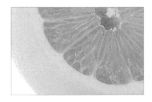

009 **Seared Squid Salad**

PREPARATION TIME 10 minutes, plus 2–4 hours marinating   **COOKING TIME** 2–3 minutes   **SERVES** 6

300g/10½oz frozen prepared small squid,
   thawed
handful of salad leaves
4 cherry tomatoes, quartered
½ bunch watercress, trimmed
½ cucumber, peeled, halved,
   deseeded and cut into fine strips
2 tbsp groundnut oil
1 tbsp lime juice
salt and freshly ground black pepper
1 tbsp coriander leaves, to sprinkle

MARINADE
1 tbsp groundnut oil
1 tsp sesame oil
1 tbsp lemon juice
1 red chilli, deseeded and finely chopped
1 garlic clove, crushed
sea salt

1 Remove the tentacles from the squid and reserve, then cut the squid bodies lengthways along one side to open them out flat. Using the point of a knife, score diagonal parallel lines on the squid bodies, but do not cut right through. Put into a non-metallic bowl with the tentacles.

2 Combine all the marinade ingredients and pour over the squid. Stir everything together, cover and leave to marinate in a cool place for 2–4 hours.

3 Lift the squid from the marinade and cook in a preheated griddle pan for 2–3 minutes, turning frequently, until chargrilled and cooked, but still tender.

4 Meanwhile, toss the salad leaves, tomatoes, watercress and cucumber together. Trickle over the groundnut oil and lime juice to moisten. Season.

5 Slice the squid bodies into rings and pile onto the salad. Sprinkle with coriander, then serve.

010 **Bean, Herb & Goats' Cheese Frittata**

PREPARATION TIME 10 minutes   COOKING TIME 15–20 minutes   SERVES 3–4

175g/6oz drained tinned cannellini
   beans, rinsed
4 eggs, lightly beaten
2 garlic cloves, finely chopped
2 tbsp flat-leaf parsley, chopped
olive oil, for frying
75g/2½oz goats' cheese, finely chopped
   or crumbled

2 well-flavoured tomatoes, chopped
2 tsp balsamic vinegar
1 tbsp shredded basil leaves
1½ tbsp freshly grated Parmesan cheese
salt and freshly ground black pepper

1 Stir the beans into the eggs with the garlic, parsley and seasoning.
2 Heat a thin film of oil in an 18–20cm/7½–8 inch frying pan over a high heat, pour in the egg
   mixture and spread it out evenly. Cook over a medium–low heat for 10–15 minutes until most
   of the mixture is set but the top is still creamy. Preheat the grill to high.
3 Scatter the goats' cheese over the top and cook under the preheated grill for 5 minutes until
   the cheese is bubbling.
4 Meanwhile, combine the tomatoes with the balsamic vinegar and basil.
5 Sprinkle the Parmesan over the frittata and serve in wedges, accompanied by the tomatoes.

011 Marinated Halloumi Salad

PREPARATION TIME 10 minutes, plus 1–4 hours marinating **COOKING TIME** 4 minutes **SERVES** 6

350g/12oz halloumi cheese, cut into
1-cm/½-in-thick slices
1 tbsp salted capers, well rinsed and dried
12 mixed black and green olives, pitted
flat-leaf parsley leaves, to scatter
lemon wedges, to serve

MARINADE
125ml/4fl oz/½ cup extra-virgin olive oil
1 tsp Dijon mustard
2 tsp balsamic vinegar
1 tbsp thyme leaves
pinch of caster sugar
1 red chilli, deseeded and finely chopped

1 Lay the cheese slices in a shallow non-metallic dish.

2 Combine the marinade ingredients and pour over the cheese. Turn the slices over, cover and leave in a cool place for 1–4 hours, turning the slices occasionally.

3 Lift the cheese from the marinade and cook in a dry non-stick frying pan for 2 minutes on each side, turning carefully, until golden.

4 Transfer to plates, scatter over the capers, olives and parsley, and serve immediately with the lemon wedges.

012 Spaghetti with Sun-Dried Tomatoes, Garlic & Chilli

PREPARATION TIME 5 minutes   **COOKING TIME** 12 minutes   **SERVES** 6

400g/14oz spaghetti
12–14 sun-dried tomatoes in oil, drained
    and sliced
3 garlic cloves, finely chopped

1 tbsp flat-leaf parsley, chopped
pinch of dried chilli flakes
50ml/1¾fl oz/scant ¼ cup extra-virgin
    olive oil

1 Cook the spaghetti in a large saucepan of boiling water following the packet instructions until just cooked or, al dente, and drain well
2 Meanwhile, combine the remaining ingredients in a small saucepan and warm over a low heat.
3 Toss the spaghetti with the sauce, and serve.

013 Bulgar-Stuffed Peppers

PREPARATION TIME 10 minutes **COOKING TIME** 25–30 minutes **SERVES** 4

3 tbsp bulgar

2 large red peppers, halved, deseeded and
stalk ends removed

2 tbsp milk

2 tbsp soft cheese with garlic and herbs

2 eggs, beaten

1 well-flavoured tomato, peeled,
deseeded and chopped

2 tbsp flat-leaf parsley, chopped

6 tbsp freshly grated Parmesan cheese

1 Preheat the oven to 180°C/350°F/Gas 4.

2 Pour boiling water over the bulgar and leave to soak, but don't allow it to become too soft.
Drain off the excess water thoroughly, if necessary.

3 Meanwhile, bring a pan of water to the boil. Add the pepper halves and blanch for 3 minutes.
Leave upside down on a tea towel to drain completely.

4 Stir the milk into the soft cheese until smooth, then mix in the eggs, bulgar, tomato and parsley.

5 Stand the pepper halves in a shallow ovenproof dish or tin, propping them upright with foil
if necessary. Spoon in the cheese mixture. Sprinkle over the Parmesan and bake in the
preheated oven for 20–25 minutes until the filling is just set. Do not overcook.

014 Spinach-Filled Tomatoes with Mozzarella

PREPARATION TIME 10 minutes   **COOKING TIME** 15 minutes   **SERVES** 4

4 large plum tomatoes, halved lengthways
2 tsp olive oil, plus extra for oiling
1 shallot, finely chopped
1 garlic clove, finely chopped

175g/6oz frozen spinach, thawed and
  squeezed dry
50–85g/2–3oz mozzarella cheese, sliced
salt and freshly ground black pepper

1 Carefully scoop the pulp from the tomatoes. Turn the shells upside down and leave to drain.
  Chop the tomato flesh.
2 Heat the oil in a small non stick frying pan, add the shallot and garlic and fry over a moderate
  heat until softened, stirring occasionally. Add the chopped tomato flesh and heat, stirring, until
  the moisture has evaporated. Stir in the spinach, season and heat through. Preheat the oven
  to 180°C/350°F/Gas 4.
3 Stand the tomato halves in an oiled baking tin, cut-side up. Pack the spinach mixture into the
  hollows and top with a slice of mozzarella.
4 Cook in the preheated oven for 20–25 minutes. Do not allow the tomatoes to become too soft
  otherwise they will be difficult to transfer to plates.

015 Grilled Tomato Bruschetta

PREPARATION TIME 5–10 minutes   COOKING TIME 6 minutes   SERVES 2–4

4 sun-ripened tomatoes, halved
olive oil, for brushing
1 large ciabatta, halved lengthways
4 tbsp tapenade
1 tbsp extra-virgin olive oil

1 Peppadew (bottled mild pepper piquante),
   drained and thinly sliced
small handful (about 10) basil leaves
salt and freshly ground black pepper

1 Preheat the grill to high. Brush the tomatoes with olive oil, season and cook on a grill rack under the preheated grill for 6 minutes, turning once.

2 Meanwhile, cut each length of ciabatta in half widthways and toast under the grill with the tomatoes. Remove from the grill rack and spread the cut sides with the tapenade.

3 Squash the tomatoes on to the ciabatta. Trickle the extra-virgin olive oil over the top and sprinkle with the Peppadew and basil leaves.

016 Green Caesar Salad

PREPARATION TIME 10 minutes **COOKING TIME** 5 minutes **SERVES** 4–6

1 large cos lettuce, torn into pieces

CROÛTONS
5 tbsp olive oil
2–3 slices of country bread, crusts removed,
   cut into 1-cm/½-in cubes
2 garlic cloves, lightly crushed

DRESSING
1 egg yolk
2 tsp wholegrain mustard
5 tbsp olive oil
3 garlic cloves, finely chopped
2 tbsp red wine vinegar
4–6 tbsp freshly grated Parmesan cheese
3 anchovy fillets, drained and chopped
freshly ground black pepper

1 To make the croûtons, heat the oil in a frying pan, add the bread cubes and the garlic and fry until crisp and lightly browned. Transfer to kitchen paper to drain.
2 Make the dressing by mixing the egg yolk with the mustard, then slowly pour in the oil, whisking until it is all incorporated. Add the garlic, vinegar, Parmesan, anchovy fillets and plenty of black pepper. Whisk until thoroughly mixed.
3 Just before serving, put the lettuce leaves into a bowl. Pour over the dressing and toss to combine, then add the croûtons and toss once more.

017 Marinated Courgettes with Lemon & Mint

PREPARATION TIME 10 minutes   **COOKING TIME** 3–5 minutes   **SERVES** 4–6

450g/1lb small courgettes, quartered
  lengthwise and halved
2 tsp olive oil
4 spring onions, white parts only,
  finely chopped
small mint leaves, to scatter

DRESSING
5 tbsp extra-virgin olive oil
2 tbsp lemon juice
1 garlic clove, chopped
1 tbsp mint leaves, chopped
pinch of caster sugar
salt and freshly ground black pepper

1 Put the courgettes in a bowl and toss with the olive oil.
2 Cook the courgettes in a griddle pan for 3–5 minutes, until lightly charred and softened,
  turning once.
3 Meanwhile, make the dressing by whisking the ingredients together with salt and pepper to taste.
4 Transfer the courgettes to a bowl and stir in the dressing, then cover with clingfilm and leave for
  20 minutes until cold.
5 To serve, add the spring onions, adjust the seasoning and scatter with the mint leaves.

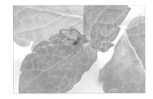

Chapter 2

FISH & SEAFOOD

Many varieties of fish have become expensive, but that does not mean you have to eliminate fish from your diet. Instead of going for the well-known varieties such as cod and haddock, look for cheaper types such as coley, pollock and huss (don't be put off by the slightly greyish colour of the first two, as they become white when cooked). When they are combined with interesting flavourings, such as Thai spices (see page 40), most people will be hard-pressed to guess that you had been saving money on the fish.

Make the most of any bargains you come across. If you see a side of salmon at a reduced price, for example, you can cut it up and freeze it. And unless you want perfect slices of smoked salmon, buy smoked salmon trimmings, which are a fraction of the price and perfect for pasta dishes, such as the one on page 34.

Seafood Linguine en Papillote (see page 49)

018 Salmon Shells with Pesto & Tomato Sauce

PREPARATION TIME 5 minutes, plus optional overnight resting and making the sauce
COOKING TIME 20–35 minutes   **SERVES** 4

200g/7oz tinned salmon, drained
100g/3½oz/scant ½ cup ricotta cheese
2–3 tsp finely grated lemon zest
16 large pasta shells
2 tbsp homemade or bought pesto

2 well-flavoured tomatoes,
   deseeded and chopped
⅔ recipe quantity Béchamel Sauce,
   (see page 90), kept warm
salt and freshly ground black pepper

1 Combine the salmon with the ricotta, lemon zest and seasoning. Cover and leave overnight,
   if time allows, to allow the flavours to develop.
2 Preheat the oven to 190°C/375°F/Gas 5.
3 Cook the pasta in a large saucepan of boiling water following the packet instructions but for
   one minute less than the suggested time. Drain well, then leave on a clean tea towel to drain
   completely.
4 Divide the salmon mixture among the shells and place, open side up, in a shallow ovenproof
   dish. Cover tightly with foil and place in the preheated oven for 15–20 minutes to warm through.
5 Add the pesto and tomatoes to the béchamel sauce and stir well. Pour the sauce over the
   shells, and serve.

019 Salmon Fishcakes

PREPARATION TIME 15 minutes, plus 2–3 hours cooling and chilling and making the sauce
COOKING TIME 20–30 minutes **SERVES** 4

450g/1lb skinless salmon fillet
350g/12oz potatoes
small knob of unsalted butter
1–2 tbsp chopped dill, to taste
juice and finely grated zest of ½ large lemon
seasoned plain flour, for shaping

2 eggs, beaten
115g/4oz/1½ cup fresh breadcrumbs
olive oil, for frying
salt and freshly ground black pepper
1 recipe quantity Red Pepper & Tomato
Sauce (see page 54), to serve

1 Put the salmon in a frying pan with barely enough water to cover. Season and bring to the boil. Remove the pan from the heat, cover and leave the salmon to cool in the liquid for one hour. Drain off the liquid. Skin the salmon and flake the flesh into a bowl.

2 Meanwhile, cook the potatoes in a saucepan of boiling salted water for 10–15 minutes until tender. Drain well, add the butter and mash.

3 Add the salmon, dill, lemon juice and zest and seasoning to the mashed potato and, with well-floured hands, form the mixture into 4 patties.

4 Tip the beaten eggs on to one plate and the breadcrumbs on to another. Coat the patties in the egg, allowing the surplus to drain off, then coat in the breadcrumbs, patting them firmly in place. Cover and chill for 1–2 hours.

5 Heat a little olive oil in a frying pan and fry the fishcakes over a moderate heat for 4 minutes on each side until golden, turning them carefully with a fish slice. Remove and drain on some kitchen paper.

6 Serve the fishcakes with the pepper and tomato sauce on the side.

020 Teriyaki Salmon

PREPARATION TIME 5 minutes, plus 1–2 hours marinating   **COOKING TIME** 4–5 minutes   **SERVES** 4

4 salmon steaks, about 175g/6oz each
lightly toasted sesame seeds, lightly
   crushed, to sprinkle

MARINADE
2 tbsp mirin
2 tbsp soy sauce
2 tbsp saké
2 tsp grated fresh root ginger
1 garlic clove, pressed through a garlic press
½–¾ tsp Sichuan peppercorns, ground

1 Place the salmon steaks in a non-metallic dish.
2 Make the marinade by mixing all the ingredients together. Pour over the salmon, turn the steaks
  over to make sure they are evenly coated, then cover and leave in a cool place for 1–2 hours,
  turning occasionally. (If marinating in the fridge, remove the salmon 30 minutes before cooking.)
3 Preheat the grill to high. Lift the steaks from the marinade. Reserve the marinade.
4 Cook the salmon on an oiled grill rack under the preheated grill for about 2 minutes, then brush
  with the reserved marinade, turn the steaks over, brush again with the marinade and cook for
  a further 2 minutes, until the salmon is cooked to your liking. Sprinkle the salmon with the
  sesame seeds before serving.

021 Couscous with Salmon, Broad Beans & Parsley

PREPARATION TIME 10–15 minutes   COOKING TIME 1 minute   SERVES 4

400g/14oz/2¼ cups couscous
175g/6oz/about 1 cup fresh or frozen
  broad beans, thawed
olive oil, for frying
2 garlic cloves, finely chopped

425g/15oz tinned salmon,
  drained and flaked
4 tbsp chopped flat-leaf parsley
about 4 tbsp lemon juice
freshly grated pecorino cheese,
  to serve (optional)

1 Put the couscous in a bowl, cover with water according to the packet instructions and leave for 5–10 minutes, adding the broad beans at the same time.

2 Meanwhile, heat a little olive oil in a small pan and fry the garlic over a low heat for 1 minute. Add to the couscous and broad beans and stir in the salmon, then toss with the parsley and lemon juice to taste. Serve with pecorino, if desired.

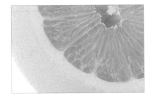

022 Green & White Tagliatelle with Smoked Salmon, Spinach & Lemon

PREPARATION TIME 5 minutes   COOKING TIME 10–12 minutes   SERVES 4

400g/14oz green and white tagliatelle
400g/14oz spinach leaves, torn into
  small pieces
small knob of unsalted butter
juice and finely grated zest of 1 lemon

200g/7oz/scant 1 cup crème fraîche
175g/6oz smoked salmon trimmings,
  cut into strips
salt and freshly ground black pepper
snipped chives, to sprinkle

1 Cook the pasta in a large saucepan of boiling water following the packet instructions until just cooked or al dente, pushing the spinach into the water 30 seconds before the end of the cooking time. Drain well.

2 Meanwhile, melt the butter in a small saucepan. Whisk in the lemon juice and zest, the crème fraîche and seasoning and warm through. Toss with the pasta, spinach and smoked salmon. Serve sprinkled with the chives.

023 Tuna & Broccoli Bake

PREPARATION TIME 10 minutes   COOKING TIME 35–40 minutes   SERVES 4

550g/1lb 4oz potatoes, halved or quartered, depending on size
175g/6oz broccoli, divided into small florets
200g/7oz tinned tuna, drained and flaked
1 large (or 2 halves) grilled red pepper in oil, drained and sliced

115g/4oz Taleggio or Fontina cheese, grated
570ml/20 fl oz/scant 2⅓ cups milk
3 eggs, beaten
2 tbsp fresh breadcrumbs
salt and freshly ground black pepper

1 Preheat the oven to 180°C/350°F/Gas 4.
2 Cook the potatoes in a saucepan of boiling salted water until tender. Drain well, then, when cool enough to handle, slice thinly. Meanwhile, cook the broccoli in a saucepan of boiling salted water until just tender, then drain well. Distribute the potatoes, broccoli, tuna, red pepper and half of the Taleggio in an oiled ovenproof dish.
3 Beat the milk with the eggs and seasoning and pour the mixture into the dish. It should flow through the ingredients, but if it does not, ease them apart with a fork. Scatter the remaining Taleggio and the breadcrumbs over the top, making sure any protruding broccoli is covered.
4 Bake in the preheated oven for about 25 minutes until just set and golden.

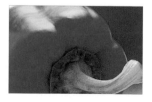

024 Rosemary-Skewered Pollock

PREPARATION TIME 5 minutes   COOKING TIME 35–40 minutes   SERVES 6

12 rosemary stalks, leaves stripped

650g/1lb 7oz pollock fillet, skinned and
  cut into chunks

1 tsp pimentón (smoked paprika)

6 slices firm white bread

salt and freshly ground black pepper

lemon wedges, to serve

GARLIC & LEMON BASTE

240ml/8fl oz/scant 1 cup olive oil

2 large garlic bulbs, divided into cloves,
  unpeeled

1 lemon, halved and cut into chunks

3 rosemary sprigs

1 To make the baste, put all the ingredients in a saucepan with some black pepper and cook
  over a very low heat for 30 minutes; do not let the oil become too hot or the garlic will fry.
  Strain off and reserve the oil and the garlic.

2 Preheat the grill to high. Using the rosemary stalks as skewers, carefully pierce a hole
  through each chunk of fish. Sprinkle the fish with black pepper and pimentón, then brush
  with the garlic-flavoured oil. Thread on to the rosemary "skewers".

3 Cook the fish on an oiled grill rack under the preheated grill for about 6–8 minutes, turning
  occasionally and brushing with some of the garlic oil, until browned at the edges. Remove
  from the grill rack and sprinkle with salt.

4 Meanwhile, toast the bread in batches and cut in half diagonally. Using a slotted spoon,
  lift the garlic from the oil and either squash the garlic flesh from the skins on to the toasts,
  or remove the skins and eat the cloves with the fish. Serve the lemon wedges on the side.

025 Haddock with Indian Spices

PREPARATION TIME 10 minutes, plus 1 hour marinating   COOKING TIME 6–8 minutes   SERVES 4

4 haddock fillets, about 200g/7oz each

MARINADE
2 tsp garam masala
1 tsp ground cumin
½ tsp chilli powder
½ tsp turmeric
3 tbsp chopped coriander
1–2 tbsp groundnut oil
salt and freshly ground black pepper

RAITA
½ cucumber, deseeded
1 small garlic clove, finely chopped
150ml/5fl oz/scant ⅔ cup Greek yogurt
2 tbsp chopped mint
salt and freshly ground black pepper

1 Put the haddock into a non-metallic dish.
2 Make the marinade by stirring all the ingredients together. Rub into the haddock to coat evenly and thoroughly. Cover and leave in the fridge to marinate for 1 hour.
3 Preheat the grill to high.To make the raita, grate the cucumber on the coarse side of a cheese grater. Drain on kitchen paper. Combine the cucumber with the garlic, yogurt, mint and seasoning.
4 Cook the haddock on an oiled grill rack under the preheated grill for 6–8 minutes until cooked through, turning once with a fish slice. Serve with the Raita.

026 Mexican Whole Fish Burgers

PREPARATION TIME 10 minutes, plus 30 minutes marinating COOKING TIME 6–8 minutes SERVES 6

850g/1lb 14oz thick, firm white fish fillets,
   such as pollock or haddock
1 bunch coriander, coarsely chopped
1 garlic clove, chopped
1 red chilli, deseeded and chopped
2 tsp paprika
1 tsp ground cumin
finely grated zest of 1 lime
5 tbsp olive oil

6 hamburger buns or rolls, split
salt and freshly ground black pepper
spinach leaves and red onion slices, to serve

LIME MAYONNAISE
115ml/3¾fl oz/scant ½ cup homemade or
   bought mayonnaise
2 tbsp lime juice
dash Tabasco sauce

1 Cut the fish into 6 pieces that are slightly larger than the buns. Put into a non-metallic dish.
2 Mix the coriander, garlic, chilli, paprika, cumin, lime zest and olive oil in a blender. Season to taste. Coat the fish evenly with the paste, then cover and leave in a cool place for 30 minutes.
3 Preheat the grill to high. Meanwhile, mix the lime mayonnaise ingredients together. Adjust the seasoning, if necessary.
4 Cook the fish under the grill on an oiled rack of a grill pan for 3–4 minutes over a moderate heat on each side until cooked through and opaque, turning with a fish slice.
5 While the fish is cooking, toast the halved buns. Spread some of the mayo on the cut sides of the buns, add some spinach leaves and red onion slices to the bases of the buns, and top with a piece of fish. Cover with the bun tops and serve.

027 Thai Fishcakes

PREPARATION TIME 10 minutes, plus 1 hour chilling   COOKING TIME 8–10 minutes   SERVES 4

1 shallot, coarsely chopped
1 plump garlic clove, coarsely chopped
1-cm/½-in piece fresh root ginger,
   coarsely chopped
2 kaffir lime leaves, or 1 tsp lime zest
1 red chilli, deseeded and coarsely chopped
2 tbsp Thai fish sauce
pinch of caster sugar

450g/1lb pollock or hake fillets,
   skinned and chopped
2 spring onions, coarsely chopped
2 tbsp finely chopped coriander, plus
   extra to sprinkle
olive oil, for frying
lime wedges, to serve

1 Combine the shallot, garlic, ginger, lime leaves, chilli, fish sauce and sugar in a food processor.
   Add the fish and process until reduced to a paste.
2 Add the spring onions and coriander. Pulse a few times until combined but not chopped further.
3 Knead the mixture with your hands until smooth, then form into 2.5-cm/1-in-thick patties.
   Chill for at least 1 hour.
4 Heat a little olive oil in a frying pan and fry the fishcakes over a moderate heat for 4–5 minutes
   on each side until golden on the outside but still rare to medium in the centre, turning them
   carefully with a fish slice. Remove and drain on kitchen paper. Sprinkle with coriander and
   serve with lime wedges.

028 Baked Trout with Fennel & Lemon

PREPARATION TIME 15 minutes   COOKING TIME 15-20 minutes   SERVES 4

1 fennel bulb

2 large trout, about 700g/1lb 9oz each, filleted to give 4 fillets

3 garlic cloves, thinly sliced

2 tbsp chopped flat-leaf parsley

1 lemon, halved and thinly sliced

1 tsp fennel seeds

1 tbsp olive oil

salt and freshly ground black pepper

1 Trim the stalks from the fennel bulb, saving the feathery green fronds. Discard the core. Halve the fennel bulb and slice thinly. Blanch in boiling salted water for 2 minutes. Drain very well.

2 Preheat the oven to 180°C/350°F/Gas 4.

3 Cut 4 sheets of foil, each large enough to enclose a fillet. Put a quarter of the garlic, sliced fennel and parsley on each sheet of foil, spreading them in an even layer. Lay a fillet on top, skinside uppermost. Lay the lemon slices on top. Scatter over the fennel seeds and reserved feathery fronds. Season and trickle the oil over the top. Fold the foil loosely over the fish and twist the edges together firmly to seal.

4 Place all the packages on a baking sheet and bake in the oven for 15–20 minutes until the flesh flakes easily with a fork.

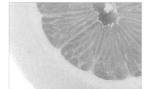

029 Whole Chinese-Style Trout

PREPARATION TIME 10 minutes, plus 2–3 hours marinating   **COOKING TIME** 15–20 minutes   **SERVES** 4

4 whole trout, cleaned
6 tbsp grated fresh root ginger
115ml/3¾fl oz/scant ½ cup rice
    wine vinegar

6 tbsp sesame oil
12 spring onions, finely chopped
several coriander sprigs
salt and freshly ground black pepper

1 Cut 2 or 3 slashes in both sides of the fish, going right down to the bone. Insert a small amount of the ginger in each slash. Season inside and out and transfer the fish to a large ovenproof dish.

2 Pour over the rice wine vinegar and sesame oil and sprinkle over the spring onions. Lay coriander sprigs on top of and around the fish. Cover with a lid or foil and leave in the fridge for about 2 hours to marinate, turning the fish over once. Preheat the oven to 180°C/350°F/ Gas 4. Bring the fish back to room temperature.

3 Cook in the oven for 25–30 minutes until the flesh in the slashes is opaque. Serve the fish with the cooking juices spooned over and accompanied by lime wedges.

030 Mackerel with Sweet Chilli & Mint

PREPARATION TIME 6 minutes   **COOKING TIME** 10–15 minutes   **SERVES** 4

4 mackerel fillets, about 200g/7oz each,
cleaned

DRESSING
3 tbsp rice wine vinegar
2 tbsp caster sugar

1½ tbsp chopped mint
1 large red chilli, deseeded and
finely chopped
5-cm/2-in piece fresh root ginger,
finely chopped

1 Preheat the grill to high.
2 Place the fillets skin-side down in an oiled shallow ovenproof dish and season. Cook under the grill for 2-3 minutes on each side until the mackerel is cooked through and the flesh flakes easily.
3 Meanwhile, make the dressing. Whisk the vinegar with the sugar, then stir in the remaining ingredients. Serve with the mackerel.

031 Smoked Fish Pie

PREPARATION TIME 15 minutes, plus making the sauces   COOKING TIME 40–45 minutes   SERVES 4–6

675–900g/1½-2lb potatoes, halved or
   quartered, depending on size
5 tbsp hot milk
50g/2oz butter, melted
350g/12oz frozen spinach, thawed and
   well drained
small knob of unsalted butter

675g/1lb 8oz smoked haddock fillet,
   skinned and cubed
2 tbsp chopped mixed herbs, such as basil,
   oregano, thyme and fennel
1 recipe quantity Béchamel Sauce
   (see page 90)
1 tbsp fresh breadcrumbs

1 Cook the potatoes in a saucepan of boiling salted water for 10–15 minutes until tender, then
   drain thoroughly. Return to the pan over a low heat for a few minutes to dry them. Add the
   milk and butter and mash the potatoes.
2 While the potatoes are cooking, squeeze out the surplus moisture from the spinach. Put
   in a pan with the unsalted butter and heat through, then spread in the bottom of a 2.5-litre/
   87-fl oz/10-cup baking dish.
3 Preheat the oven to 190ºC/375ºF/Gas 5. Arrange the haddock over the spinach. Stir the herbs
   into the béchamel sauce and pour over the haddock. Spread the mashed potatoes evenly over
   the sauce and sprinkle with the breadcrumbs. Bake in the preheated oven for about 30
   minutes until golden and bubbling.

032 Fish Tortillas with Tomato & Coriander Salsa

PREPARATION TIME 15 minutes   COOKING TIME 6 minutes   SERVES 4

1 garlic clove, crushed to a paste

½ tsp ground cumin

½ tsp dried oregano

½ tsp hot paprika

1 tbsp lime juice

2 tbsp olive oil, plus extra for frying

600g/1lb 5oz pollock fillets

8 soft flour tortillas

8 tbsp homemade or bought mayonnaise

salt and freshly ground black pepper

SALSA

4 vine-ripened tomatoes, deseeded and diced

1 small red onion, finely chopped

2 tbsp chopped coriander

1 red chilli, deseeded and finely chopped

1 tbsp lemon juice

1 Make the salsa by combing the ingredients in a non metallic bowl. Cover and set aside.

2 Mix the crushed garlic with a pinch of salt, some black pepper, the spices, lime juice and olive oil. Brush the fish with the mixture.

3 Cook the fish in a little oil in a frying pan for 3 minutes on each side, then transfer to a plate.

4 Meanwhile, warm the tortillas according to the packet instructions.

5 Flake the fish coarsely with a fork and serve in the tortillas with the salsa and some mayonnaise.

033 Spiced Sardines with Orange & Olive Salad

PREPARATION TIME 15 minutes, plus 2–3 hours marinating   **COOKING TIME** 6–8 minutes   **SERVES** 4

4 garlic cloves, crushed

1 tbsp olive oil

1 tbsp lemon juice

1 tsp ground Sichuan peppercorns

½ tsp hot paprika

12–16 fresh sardines, depending on size, cleaned

salt and freshly ground black pepper

SALAD

5 oranges

1 small red onion, very thinly sliced

16 large salt-packed black olives, pitted

25g/1oz flat-leaf parsley leaves, coarsely chopped

extra virgin olive oil, for trickling

1 Mix together the garlic, olive oil, lemon juice, peppercorns, paprika and seasoning. Rub thoroughly over the sardines, then cover and leave in a cool place for 2–3 hours.

2 Preheat the grill to high. Make the salad by peeling and segmenting the oranges, removing all the pith and membranes. Put the segments in a bowl with the red onion, olives and parsley. Season and trickle over some oil.

3 Thread the sardines on to pairs of oiled parallel skewers, alternating the heads and tails, and cook on an oiled grill rack under the preheated grill for 3–4 minutes on each side. Serve with the orange and olive salad.

034 Spaghetti with Prawns, Tomatoes & Capers

PREPARATION TIME 10 minutes   **COOKING TIME** 10–12 minutes   **SERVES** 4

400g/14oz spaghetti
1 onion, chopped
olive oil, for frying
2 garlic cloves, crushed
500g/1lb 2oz ripe well-flavoured plum
   tomatoes, chopped

1 tsp oregano
350g/12oz frozen medium raw peeled
   prawns, thawed
1½ tbsp salted capers, rinsed and dried
salt and freshly ground black pepper

1 Cook the spaghetti in a large saucepan of boiling water following the packet instructions until just cooked, or al dente.

2 Meanwhile, fry the onion in a little oil in a large frying pan over a moderate heat until softened and beginning to colour. Add the garlic and fry for 1–2 minutes. Add the tomatoes and oregano and cook over a high heat until the juice has evaporated, but do not let the tomatoes disintegrate.

3 Add the prawns to the sauce and cook over a reduced heat for about 2 minutes, just until they turn pink. Remove the pan from the heat and add the capers and seasoning.

4 Drain the spaghetti, toss with the sauce and serve.

035 Seafood Linguine en Papillote

PREPARATION TIME 5 minutes **COOKING TIME** 30–35 minutes **SERVES** 4–6

500g/1lb 2oz linguine

olive oil, for frying

2 garlic cloves, crushed

400g/14oz/1⅔ cups tinned tomatoes

2 tbsp sun-dried tomato paste

700g/1lb 9oz frozen mixed seafood, thawed

1½–2 tbsp capers

leaves from a small bunch of flat-leaf parsley, chopped

salt and freshly ground black pepper

1 Preheat the oven to 190°C/375°F/Gas 5. Lightly oil 4 or 6 pieces of greaseproof paper, each 35-cm/14-in square.

2 Cook the linguine in a large saucepan of boiling water following the packet instructions, but for 1 minute less than the suggested time.

3 Meanwhile, heat a little oil in a saucepan and fry the garlic over a low heat for 1 minute. Stir in the tomatoes, tomato paste and seasoning, increase the heat and bring to the boil, then reduce the heat and simmer, uncovered, for 5 minutes.

4 Drain the pasta and toss it and the seafood, capers and parsley with the tomato sauce.

5 Place one portion in the centre of each piece of greaseproof paper. Fold the edges loosely over the pasta mixture and twist the edges together to seal tightly. Place on a baking sheet and cook in the preheated oven for 20–25 minutes until hot throughout.

036 Fusilli with Mussels, Tomatoes & Chilli

PREPARATION TIME 15 minutes   COOKING TIME 12–15 minutes   SERVES 4

400g/14oz fusilli
4 tbsp medium-bodied dry white wine
900g/2lb mussels, scrubbed, cleaned and
  thoroughly rinsed
3 tbsp olive oil
2 garlic cloves, finely chopped

1 small red chilli, deseeded and
  finely chopped
300g/10oz well-flavoured cherry tomatoes
leaves from a small bunch of flat-leaf
  parsley, chopped
salt and freshly ground black pepper

1 Cook the pasta in a large saucepan of boiling water following the packet instructions until just
  cooked or al dente.
2 Meanwhile, put the wine and mussels (discarding any that don't shut when tapped) in a large
  saucepan, cover and cook over a medium heat for 3–4 minutes, shaking the pan frequently,
  until the shells open; discard any that remain closed.
3 While the pasta and mussels are cooking, heat the oil in a large frying pan and fry the garlic
  and chilli over a low heat for about 2 minutes until soft but not coloured. Halve some of the
  tomatoes, then add all the tomatoes to the pan and fry until just beginning to soften.
4 Remove the shells from half of the mussels and strain off and reserve the cooking liquid. Add
  the parsley, all the mussels, the reserved cooking liquid and seasoning to the tomato sauce and
  heat through gently. Drain the pasta, toss with the sauce and and serve.

037 Spaghetti alla Puttanesca

PREPARATION TIME 5 minutes **COOKING TIME** 20 minutes **SERVES** 4

olive oil, for frying
2 garlic cloves, chopped
6 tinned anchovy fillets, drained
  and chopped
800g/1lb 12oz/3⅓ cups tinned
  chopped tomatoes

450g/1lb spaghetti
1 tbsp oregano
1 tbsp capers, rinsed
14 oil-cured pitted black olives, sliced
salt and freshly ground black pepper

1 Heat a little oil in a frying pan and fry the garlic over a low heat for 1 minute, then stir in the anchovy fillets until they have disintegrated. Add the tomatoes and bring to the boil, then reduce the heat and simmer for about 15 minutes, uncovered, stirring occasionally, until the sauce has thickened. Season with plenty of black pepper.

2 Meanwhile, cook the spaghetti in a large saucepan of boiling water following the packet instructions until just cooked or al dente and drain well.

3 Add the oregano, capers and olives to the sauce, and toss with the pasta.

Chapter 3

POULTRY & MEAT

You'll find that frozen meat and poultry are much cheaper than the fresh versions, and by using seasonings and flavourings imaginatively, you can make truly delicious dishes. Turkey is a particularly economical buy, and a flavoursome marinade can transform it into a really tasty dish, as shown in the Turkey Steaks with Garlic, Ginger & Sesame on page 68.

To make meat and poultry go further, you can combine them with less expensive ingredients such as pulses. A dish that illustrates this is the Sausage & Mushroom Casserole on page 71. Here you can use one can of beans if you are making it for four people but two cans and no extra meat if there are six people to feed. Pasta dishes are also a way of making a little expensive protein go a long way, and they are almost always popular.

Sausage & Aubergine Lasagne (see page 74)

038 Chicken-Stuffed Pasta Shells

PREPARATION TIME 15 minutes   COOKING TIME 45 minutes–1 hour   SERVES 4

225g/8oz button mushrooms, sliced
1 onion, finely chopped
175g/6oz courgettes, finely chopped
1 red pepper, halved, deseeded and
    finely chopped
olive oil, for frying
115g/4oz frozen skinless, boneless chicken
    breast, thawed and finely chopped
15g/½oz/¼ cup fresh breadcrumbs
2 tbsp chopped flat-leaf parsley
3 tbsp chicken stock

16 large pasta shells, about 5.5cm/2¼in
    long
salt and freshly ground black pepper

RED PEPPER & TOMATO SAUCE
2 large red peppers (about 225g/8oz each),
    halved, deseeded and chopped
1 garlic clove, chopped
2 spring onions, chopped
350g/12oz ripe tomatoes, chopped
leaves from a small bunch of basil, shredded

1 Fry the mushrooms, onion, courgettes and pepper in a little oil in a frying pan over a moderate
   heat, stirring occasionally, until softened. Stir in the chicken and cook for a further 5 minutes.
   Add the breadcrumbs, parsley, stock and seasoning and bring to the boil, then set aside.
2 Cook the pasta shells in a large saucepan of boiling water following the packet instructions,
   but for 1 minute less than the suggested time.
3 Meanwhile, make the sauce by cooking the peppers, garlic, spring onions and tomatoes
   in a saucepan for 15–20 minutes, uncovered, until thickened. Pour into a blender or food
   processor and blend until almost smooth, or use a stick blender. Add the basil and season.
4 Preheat the oven to 220°C/425°F/Gas 7.
5 Drain the pasta shells well. Fill with the chicken mixture and arrange in a single layer in a
   shallow ovenproof dish. Pour the sauce around. Cover and bake in the preheated oven for
   15 minutes, or until hot and bubbling

039 Chicken with Lemon & Mustard Sauce

PREPARATION TIME 10 minutes, plus 2 hours marinating   COOKING TIME 15–20 minutes   SERVES 4

8 chicken thighs

MARINADE
2 plump garlic cloves
3 tbsp Dijon mustard

5 tbsp olive oil
5 tbsp lemon juice
½ tsp dried thyme
salt and freshly ground black pepper

1 Cut slashes in the chicken, then arrange in a single layer in an ovenproof dish.
2 Crush the garlic to a paste with a pinch of salt, using the back of a knife. Mix with the remaining ingredients. Spread evenly over the chicken and turn the pieces over to ensure they are evenly coated, then cover and leave in a cool place for 2 hours, turning occasionally.
3 Preheat the oven to 180°C/350°F/Gas 4, or preheat the grill. Cook the chicken pieces for about 20 minutes, or grill for about 15 minutes, turning occasionally, until the skin is golden and the juices run clear when the thickest part is pierced with a skewer.

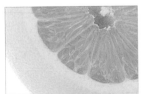

040 Tandoori Chicken Kebabs

PREPARATION TIME 10 minutes, plus 2 hours marinating   **COOKING TIME** 10 minutes   **SERVES** 4

8 boneless chicken thighs, cut into
approximately 2.5-cm/1-in pieces

MARINADE
225ml/7¾fl oz/scant 1 cup natural yogurt
2 garlic cloves, finely chopped
2 tsp grated fresh root ginger

½ red chilli, deseeded and finely chopped
1 tsp ground cardamom
1 tsp ground coriander
1 tsp garam masala
1 tsp ground cumin
salt

1 Put the chicken in a shallow, non-metallic dish.
2 Make the marinade by stirring the ingredients together and season with salt. Pour over the
   chicken and turn the pieces over to ensure they are coated thoroughly and evenly. Cover and
   leave to chill for 2 hours, turning occasionally.
3 Preheat the grill to high. Drain the chicken from the marinade and thread on to skewers
   (soaked if wooden). Cook the chicken on an oiled grill rack under the preheated grill for about
   10 minutes, turning occasionally, until browned and the juices run clear when the thickest
   part is pierced with a skewer.

041 Chicken with Ginger, Garam Masala & Coconut

PREPARATION TIME 10 minutes   COOKING TIME 12–15 minutes   SERVES 4

olive oil, for frying
1 onion, chopped
4 garlic cloves, crushed
1 tbsp grated fresh root ginger
8 boneless chicken thighs or drumsticks,
    cut into bite-sized pieces

1 tbsp garam masala
100ml/3½fl oz/scant 1 cup coconut milk
1 tbsp Thai fish sauce
1 small handful coriander leaves
freshly ground black pepper

1 Heat a little oil in a frying pan over a low heat and cook the onion and garlic for a few minutes until softened. Add the ginger and stir for 1–2 minutes, then add the chicken. Stir for about 2 minutes, then sprinkle in the garam masala and stir again before mixing in the coconut milk and fish sauce.

2 Season with pepper and bring just to the boil, then reduce the heat and simmer gently, covered, for 5–7 minutes until the chicken is cooked through. Scatter the coriander over the dish and serve.

042 Moroccan Chicken with Tabbouleh

PREPARATION TIME 15 minutes, plus 2–5 hours marinating   COOKING TIME 8 minutes   SERVES 4

800g/1lb 12oz frozen chicken breasts,
   thawed and cut into 2.5-cm/1-in pieces
2 tbsp olive oil
5 tbsp lemon juice
1 plump garlic clove, finely chopped
small handful coriander, finely chopped
small handful flat-leaf parsley, finely chopped
1 tbsp ground cumin
1 tbsp cinnamon
1 tbsp ground coriander
salt and freshly ground black pepper

TABBOULEH
115g/4oz/⅔ cup bulgar
115g/4oz Italian mixed peppers in oil,
   drained and chopped
4 tbsp olive oil
4 tbsp lemon juice
2 handfuls flat-leaf parsley, finely chopped
8 large sprigs of mint, finely chopped

1 Thread the chicken pieces on to skewers (soaked if wooden) and place in a single layer in
   a non-metallic dish.
2 Combine the olive oil, lemon juice, garlic, herbs, spices and seasoning. Pour over the chicken
   pieces and turn to ensure they are well coated, then cover and leave to marinate in a cool
   place for 2–5 hours.
3 Meanwhile, make the tabbouleh by putting the bulgar into a heatproof bowl. Pour over
   115ml/3¾fl oz/scant ½ cup boiling water and leave for 30 minutes until the water has
   been absorbed, stirring occasionally.
4 Preheat the grill to high. Fluff up the bulgar with a fork. Stir through the remaining
   tabbouleh ingredients and season.
5 Lift the chicken from the dish (reserving the marinade) and cook on an oiled grill rack
   under the preheated grill for 4 minutes on each side, brushing with the reserved marinade
   occasionally. Using a fork, slip the cooked chicken from the skewers on to the tabbouleh.

043 Turkish Chicken Wraps

PREPARATION TIME 10 minutes, plus 1–3 hours marinating   **COOKING TIME** 14–16 minutes   **SERVES** 4

4 frozen skinless, boneless chicken
  breasts, thawed
2 garlic cloves
½ tsp cinnamon
½ tsp ground allspice
4 tbsp Greek yogurt
3 tbsp lemon juice
1 tbsp olive oil
4 pitta breads
salt and freshly ground black pepper

shredded iceberg lettuce and sliced
  tomatoes, to serve

CORIANDER AÏOLI
3 garlic cloves, chopped
2 egg yolks
juice of 1 lime, or to taste
300ml/10½fl oz/scant 1¼ cups
  groundnut oil
small handful coriander leaves, chopped

1 Put the chicken into a non-metallic dish. Crush the garlic with a pinch of salt, using the back of a
  knife, then mix with the spices, yogurt, lemon juice, oil and black pepper. Coat the chicken evenly
  with the mixture. Cover and leave to marinate in a cool place for 1–3 hours, turning occasionally.
2 To make the aïoli, put the garlic, egg yolks and lime juice into a blender and mix briefly. With the
  motor running, slowly pour in the oil until the mixture becomes thick and creamy. Season and
  transfer to a bowl. Cover and chill, until ready to serve. Bring to room temperature for 30 minutes
  before serving, if desired. Stir in the coriander.
3 Preheat the grill to medium-high. Lift the chicken from the marinade. Cook on an oiled grill rack
  under the preheated grill for about 7–8 minutes on each side. Remove, cover and set aside for
  5–10 minutes before slicing.
4 Meanwhile, warm the pittas under the preheated grill for 30 seconds per side. Split each one
  open and stack the halves on top of each other, cut side uppermost. Divide the lettuce and
  tomatoes over the pitta stacks. Lay the chicken on top, add some aïoli and roll them up.

044 Peking-Style Chicken

PREPARATION TIME 15 minutes, plus 4–6 hours marinating   COOKING TIME 45 minutes   SERVES 4

1.5kg/3lb 6oz frozen chicken breasts on the
  bone, thawed
1 bunch spring onions, sliced
Chinese pancakes, to serve

DIPPING SAUCE
2 tsp sesame oil
2.5cm/1in piece fresh root ginger, grated
115ml/3¾fl oz/scant ½ cup hoisin sauce

GLAZE
2 tbsp hoisin sauce
2 tbsp white wine vinegar
2 tbsp clear honey
2 tbsp mango chutney
1 tbsp soy sauce
juice of 1 lemon

1 Make the glaze by stirring all the ingredients together in a bowl. Brush evenly and thoroughly over the chicken and place in a single layer in a shallow ovenproof dish. Cover and leave in a cool place for 4–6 hours, brushing occasionally with any remaining glaze.

2 Preheat the oven to 180°C/350°F/Gas 4. Make the dipping sauce by heating the sesame oil in a small saucepan. Add the ginger and cook over a low heat for 5 minutes. Put the hoisin sauce in a small dish, strain in the oil and stir to combine.

3 Uncover the baking dish and cook the chicken in the preheated oven for about 40 minutes, turning occasionally, until the juices run clear when the thickest part is pierced. Remove from the oven and leave to stand for 5 minutes before slicing the meat.

4 Meanwhile, warm the pancakes following the packet instructions. Serve the sliced chicken, spring onions, pancakes and dipping sauce separately so that everyone can assemble their own.

045 Jerk Chicken

PREPARATION TIME 10 minutes, plus 2 hours marinating   **COOKING TIME** 35 minutes   **SERVES** 6

6 whole chicken legs

JERK SAUCE
1 onion, coarsely chopped
115ml/3¾fl oz/scant ½ cup white wine
   vinegar
115ml/3¾fl oz/scant ½ cup dark soy sauce

50g/2oz fresh root ginger, coarsely chopped
leaves from small bunch of thyme
1–2 red chillies, deseeded and
   finely chopped
½ tsp ground allspice
freshly ground black pepper

1 Put the chicken in a large, shallow ovenproof dish.
2 Make the jerk sauce by combining the ingredients in a blender until smooth. Pour evenly over the chicken and turn the pieces over to ensure they are evenly coated, then cover and leave in a cool place for 2 hours, turning occasionally.
3 Preheat the oven to 180°C/350°F/Gas 4. Cook the chicken pieces for about 35 minutes, turning occasionally, until the skin is golden and the juices run clear when the thickest part is pierced with a skewer.

046 Chicken Curry

PREPARATION TIME 10 minutes   COOKING TIME 30 minutes   SERVES 4

olive oil, for frying
1 onion, finely chopped
4 frozen chicken breasts, thawed

COCONUT SAUCE
2 tsp cumin seeds
1 red chilli, deseeded and coarsely chopped
3 garlic cloves, coarsely chopped

½ tsp salt
1 lemongrass stem, outer layer removed,
    thinly sliced
375ml/13fl oz/scant 1½ cups coconut milk
2 tbsp lime juice
3 tbsp chopped coriander
3 tbsp chopped flat-leaf parsley

1 To make the coconut sauce, heat a small, dry, heavy-based frying pan, add the cumin seeds
   and heat for about 10 seconds until fragrant. Tip into a small blender or food processor, add
   the chilli, garlic, salt and lemongrass and mix together. Add the coconut milk, lime juice,
   coriander and parsley and process to a smooth sauce.
2 Heat a little oil in a frying pan and fry the onion until softened, then add the chicken breasts
   and seal on both sides. Pour the coconut sauce over the top and bring to the boil, then reduce
   the heat and simmer very gently, uncovered, for 20–25 minutes until the sauce has thickened
   and the chicken is cooked through and the juices run clear when the thickest part is pierced.

047 Mushroom-Stuffed Chicken Thighs

PREPARATION TIME 10 minutes, plus 20 minutes soaking the cocktail sticks   **COOKING TIME** 15 minutes
SERVES 4

15g/½oz/1 tbsp unsalted butter
50g/2oz mushrooms, finely chopped
25g/1oz full-fat soft cheese
1 tbsp chopped parsley

8 boneless chicken thighs
olive oil, for brushing
salt and freshly ground black pepper

1 Soak 8–16 wooden cocktail sticks in water for 20 minutes. Drain and set aside. Melt the butter
in a frying pan and fry the mushrooms over a moderate heat for 5 minutes until tender. Using
a slotted spoon, transfer on to a piece of kitchen paper to drain.

2 Preheat the grill to medium. Mix the mushrooms with the cheese, parsley and seasoning, and
use this mixture to stuff the chicken thighs. Secure the thighs closed with cocktail sticks. Brush
the thighs with oil and season them.

3 Cook on an oiled grill rack under the preheated grill for 10–15 minutes, turning once, until
browned and cooked through.

048 Fruited Chicken Couscous

PREPARATION TIME 10 minutes   COOKING TIME 10–15 minutes   SERVES 4

570ml/20 fl oz/2⅓ cups hot vegetable stock
225g/8oz/1¼ cups couscous
8 boneless chicken thighs or drumsticks,
   or a combination of both
750ml/26fl oz/3 cups chicken stock
75g/2½oz/½ cup dried apricots, chopped
50g/2oz/⅓ cup raisins
75g/2½oz/½ cup dried figs, chopped
40g/1½oz/scant ½ cup toasted flaked almonds

75g/2½oz/heaped ⅓ cup pistachio nuts,
   lightly toasted
4 tbsp chopped flat-leaf parsley
2 tbsp chopped coriander leaves
1 tbsp chopped mint leaves
4 tbsp olive oil
juice and finely grated zest of 1 orange
salt and freshly ground black pepper

1 Pour the vegetable stock over the couscous in a heatproof bowl, stir with a fork, cover and
   leave to cool.

2 Meanwhile, poach the chicken very gently in the chicken stock in a large saucepan for
   10–15 minutes until cooked through. Lift the chicken out of the stock, remove the skin
   and cut the meat into bite-sized pieces.

3 Fluff up the couscous with a fork, then fork in the fruits, nuts, herbs and chicken.

4 Combine the olive oil with the orange juice and zest and salt and black pepper. Whisk until
   emulsified, then stir into the couscous.

049 Cajun Chicken with Tomato Salsa

PREPARATION TIME 10 minutes, plus 2–3 hours marinating   **COOKING TIME** 15 minutes   **SERVES** 6

2 tsp dried thyme

2 tsp dried oregano

2 tsp paprika

1 tsp ground cumin

1 tsp cayenne pepper

6 frozen boneless chicken breasts,
  with skin on, thawed

groundnut oil, for brushing

salt and freshly ground black pepper

lime quarters, to serve

TOMATO SALSA

700g/1lb 9oz firm but ripe plum tomatoes,
  chopped

1 red onion, finely chopped

1 small red chilli, deseeded and finely
  chopped

1½ tbsp chopped coriander

1½ tbsp balsamic vinegar

3 tbsp olive oil

1 Mix together the herbs, spices and seasoning. Brush the chicken lightly with oil, then rub the
   spice mixture into the chicken. Cover and leave in a cool place for 2–3 hours to marinate.

2 Meanwhile, make the salsa by combining the ingredients in a non metallic bowl. Add salt to
   taste. Cover and chill.

3 Preheat the grill to medium. Thread the lime quarters on to skewers, if you would like them grilled.

4 Cook the chicken on an oiled grill rack under the preheated grill for about 15 minutes until
   browned and cooked through, turning once.
   If grilling the limes, cook the skewers
   alongside until caramelized. Serve the
   chicken with the lime quarters, either
   fresh or grilled as above, and
   accompanied by the salsa.

050 Turkey Steaks with Garlic, Ginger & Sesame

PREPARATION TIME 10 minutes, plus 4–6 hours marinating   COOKING TIME 10–12 minutes   SERVES 4

4 turkey steaks

MARINADE
3 garlic cloves, finely chopped
2 tbsp grated fresh root ginger

115ml/3¾fl oz/scant ½ cup dark soy sauce
1 tbsp rice wine or medium sherry
1 tbsp sesame oil
2 tsp sesame seeds
2 tbsp dark brown sugar

1 Using the point of a sharp knife, make cuts over the top and bottom of the turkey steaks.
   Lay the steaks in a single layer in a non-metallic dish.
2 Put the marinade ingredients in a jug or bowl and mix to combine, then pour evenly over the
   steaks, turning them over to coat thoroughly. Cover and leave in a cool place for 4–6 hours
   to marinate, turning occasionally.
3 Lift the turkey steaks from the marinade and cook in a preheated griddle pan for 5–6 minutes
   on each side until the juices run clear when the thickest part is pierced with a skewer.

051 Turkey Tikka Sausages

PREPARATION TIME 10 minutes, plus 4 hours chilling (optional), plus making the raita
COOKING TIME 12–16 minutes   SERVES 4

olive oil, for frying
1 onion, finely chopped
500g/1lb 2oz minced turkey
4 tbsp tikka masala paste
3 tbsp chopped coriander

2 tbsp natural yogurt
1 tbsp mango chutney
salt and freshly ground black pepper
4 small naan breads and 1 recipe quantity
Raita (see page 38), to serve

1 Heat a little oil in a frying pan, add the onion and fry over a moderate heat until softened. Remove from the heat and leave to cool.

2 Put all the remaining ingredients in a bowl and mix until thoroughly combined. With wet hands, form the mixture into 4 sausages. If possible, cover and leave in a cool place for 4 hours or overnight to allow the flavours to develop.

3 Preheat the grill to medium. Cook the sausages on an oiled grill rack under the preheated grill for 6–8 minutes on each side until the juices run clear, turning them carefully with a fish slice.

4 Remove the sausages and warm the naan breads for 20–30 seconds under the grill. Serve the sausages with the naan breads and raita.

052 Potatoes with Chorizo, Rocket & Tomatoes

PREPARATION TIME 5 minutes   COOKING TIME 20 minutes   SERVES 2–3

450g/1lb potatoes, cut into about
   2-cm/¾-in chunks
125g/4½oz piece chorizo, chopped
olive oil, for frying
250g/9oz ripe well-flavoured tomatoes,
   halved lengthways

2 tsp balsamic vinegar
2 tbsp sun-dried tomato and
   olive tapenade
50g/2oz rocket
freshly ground black pepper

1 Cook the potatoes in a saucepan of boiling salted water for about 10 minutes until just tender.
2 Meanwhile, fry the chorizo in a little olive oil in a non-stick frying pan for 2–3 minutes. Add
   the tomatoes and balsamic vinegar and cook until the tomatoes are just beginning to collapse.
3 Drain the potatoes and coarsely chop. Stir them into the frying pan with the tapenade, then
   stir in the rocket and black pepper, and serve.

053 Sausage & Mushroom Casserole

PREPARATION TIME 10 minutes   COOKING TIME 30–35 minutes   SERVES 4–6

450g/1lb pork and herb sausages

olive oil, for frying

1 onion, finely chopped

2 garlic cloves, finely chopped

300g/10½oz mushrooms, chopped

1 tbsp thyme leaves

800g/1lb 12oz/3⅓ cups tinned tomatoes

400–800g/14oz–1lb 12oz tinned soya,

white kidney or borlotti beans, drained

and rinsed

salt and freshly ground black pepper

small handful flat-leaf parsley

1 Heat a little oil in a non-stick frying pan and fry the sausages over a moderate heat, turning them frequently, until evenly browned. Transfer to a large saucepan. (If this dish is to serve 6 people, chop the sausages at this point.) Fry the onion and garlic, adding a little extra oil if necessary, until evenly browned. Transfer to the saucepan.

2 Add the mushrooms and thyme to the frying pan and cook until the liquid from the mushrooms has evaporated, but do not let them become too dry. Season. Add to the saucepan with the tomatoes and beans (using 1 can to serve 4 or 2 cans to serve 6).

3 Bring to the boil, then reduce the heat and simmer gently, covered, for 15 minutes, then remove the lid (if there is too much liquid) and simmer for a further 5–10 minutes. (If using 2 cans of beans, leave the lid on throughout the cooking.) Scatter the parsley over the top and serve.

054 Pasta with Bacon, Tomatoes & Chilli

PREPARATION TIME 10 minutes   COOKING TIME 30 minutes   SERVES 4

olive oil, for frying
1 onion, finely chopped
115g/4oz smoked back bacon,
    cut into strips
1 garlic clove, finely chopped
pinch of chilli flakes, to taste
5 tbsp medium-bodied dry white wine

800g/1lb 12oz/3⅓ cups tinned chopped
    plum tomatoes
400g/14oz small pasta shapes
3 tbsp freshly grated Parmesan cheese,
    plus extra to serve
salt and freshly ground black pepper

1 Heat a little oil in a frying pan and fry the onion and bacon over a moderate heat until the
    bacon is brown but not crisp, and the onion is soft and turning golden. Add the garlic and
    chilli flakes towards the end of the cooking.
2 Pour in the wine and bring to the boil, then bubble until evaporated by about three-quarters.
    Add the tomatoes and continue simmering until thickened. Season to taste.
3 Meanwhile, cook the pasta in a large saucepan of boiling salted water following the packet
    instructions until just cooked, or al dente, and drain well. Toss with the sauce and the
    Parmesan and serve with additional Parmesan.

055 Potato, Chorizo & Mozzarella Torta

PREPARATION TIME 10 minutes   COOKING TIME 35–40 minutes   SERVES 4

500g/1lb 2oz potatoes, halved
3–4 tbsp olive oil
200g/7oz mozzarella cheese, very
   thinly sliced
8–12 basil leaves

100g/3½oz chorizo, very finely sliced
4 eggs, beaten
2 large red peppers, halved and deseeded
salt and freshly ground black pepper

1 Cook the potatoes in a saucepan of boiling salted water for about 10 minutes until just tender.
Drain well, then, when cool enough to handle, slice thinly.

2 Preheat the grill to high. Pour a little of the oil into a large frying pan, preferably non-stick, and
place an even layer of half the potato slices on the base. Top with the mozzarella, basil leaves,
chorizo and then the remaining potato.

3 Cook the red peppers in a grill pan under the preheated grill for 10–15 minutes until charred
and blistered. Leave until cool enough to handle, then peel off the skins and slice the flesh.

4 Meanwhile, season the eggs, then pour them over the potatoes. Cook over a medium heat for
about 8 minutes until the underneath is golden.

5 Put a large plate over the top. Flip the pan over so the torta falls on to the plate. Add a little
more oil to the pan and slide the torta back in. Cook for a further 5–6 minutes until the other
side is golden. Flip out of the pan on to a warmed serving plate. Serve in large wedges,
accompanied by the grilled red peppers.

056 Sausage & Aubergine Lasagne

PREPARATION TIME 20 minutes, plus making the sauce   COOKING TIME 50 minutes   SERVES 6

12 lasagne sheets

olive oil, for cooking the lasagne, brushing and oiling

250g/9oz sausages

375g/13oz aubergines, cut into 5-mm/¼-in slices

75g/2½oz Parmesan cheese, freshly grated

1 recipe quantity Béchamel Sauce (see page 90)

175g/6oz mozzarella cheese, sliced

375g/13oz well-flavoured tomatoes, sliced

salt and freshly ground black pepper

1 Preheat the grill to high.

2 Cook the lasagne sheets in batches in boiling salted water, to which a little oil has been added, for 3 minutes for fresh lasagne or 7 minutes for dried. Drain the lasagne, then rinse it and drain again. Spread on a clean tea towel to dry. (Follow these instructions even if using no-pre-cook lasagne.)

3 Meanwhile, grill the sausages on an oiled grill rack under the preheated grill until evenly browned. Drain on kitchen paper and then slice thinly.

4 Lay the aubergine slices in a single layer on a large baking sheet (you may need to use two sheets), brush lightly with oil and season. Grill until tender and brown red on both sides. Preheat the oven to 180°C/350°F/Gas 4.

5 Stir three-quarters of the Parmesan into the béchamel sauce, then spread a thin layer of the sauce over the bottom of an oiled ovenproof dish (about 25 x 16 x 7.5cm/10 x 6¼ x 3in). Cover with a layer of 3 lasagne sheets and arrange half the aubergine and sausage slices on top. Add a further layer of sauce, one of lasagne and then half the mozzarella. Cover with half the tomatoes, another layer of lasagne sheets, the remaining aubergines and sausages, more sauce, remaining lasagne and the rest of the mozzarella and tomatoes. Finish with a generous layer of cheese sauce. Sprinkle over the remaining Parmesan.

6 Bake in the preheated oven for about 30 minutes until bubbling and brown, then serve.

057 Spaghetti alla Carbonara

PREPARATION TIME 5 minutes   COOKING TIME 10–12 minutes   SERVES 2–3

250g/9oz spaghetti

small knob of unsalted butter

75g/2½oz smoked bacon, cut into strips

4 tbsp medium-bodied dry white wine

2 eggs

2 tbsp finely chopped flat-leaf parsley

25g/1oz pecorino cheese, freshly grated

25g/1oz Parmesan cheese, freshly grated

salt and freshly ground black pepper

1 Cook the spaghetti in a large saucepan of boiling water following the packet instructions until just cooked or al dente.

2 Meanwhile, melt the butter in a frying pan and fry the bacon until crisp. Add the wine and boil until reduced by half.

3 While the bacon is cooking, in a bowl that is large enough to hold the cooked pasta, beat the eggs with the parsley, half of each of the cheeses, a pinch of salt and plenty of black pepper.

4 Drain the pasta and immediately add it to the bowl of eggs. Quickly toss together, adding the bacon as well, until the eggs are creamy. Toss lightly with the remaining cheese and serve.

058 Gammon with Paprika Spice Rub

PREPARATION TIME 15 minutes, plus 2 hours marinating   COOKING TIME 10–12 minutes   SERVES 4

4 gammon steaks, about 175g/6oz each

2 tsp ground cumin

2 tsp paprika

4 tsp dark soft brown sugar

4 tbsp olive oil

MANGO SALSA

2 large ripe mangoes

juice of 2 limes

½ red onion, finely chopped

3 tbsp finely chopped coriander

pinch of dark soft brown sugar

salt and freshly ground black pepper

1 Trim any surplus fat from the steaks, leaving just enough to keep them moist. Snip the remaining fat at 2.5-cm/1-in intervals.

2 Mix the cumin, paprika, sugar and oil together and rub all over the gammon steaks. Cover and leave to marinate in a cool place for 2 hours.

3 Meanwhile, preheat the grill to high.Peel the mangoes, and cut the flesh away from the pit with a knife. Dice a quarter of the flesh. Purée the remaining flesh with the lime juice, then stir in the onion, coriander and diced mango. Add the sugar, and seasoning to taste.

4 Cook the gammon on an oiled grill rack under the preheated grill for 5–6 minutes on each side until the juices run clear when the thickest part is pierced with a fine skewer. Serve with the salsa.

059 Spanish Burgers

PREPARATION TIME 15 minutes, plus 4–8 hours marinating   COOKING TIME 15 minutes   SERVES 4

1 tbsp olive oil
1 onion, finely chopped
500g/1lb 2oz coarse-ground pork
75g/2½oz chorizo, finely chopped
3 tbsp chopped oregano
flour, for dusting
salt and freshly ground black pepper

MARINADE
150ml/5fl oz/scant ⅔ cup olive oil
2 garlic cloves, crushed
1 tbsp sun-dried tomato paste
1 tbsp chopped thyme
2 tsp chopped parsley

TO SERVE
4 hamburger buns or rolls, split into halves
home-made or bought mayonnaise
lettuce
chopped tomatoes
spring onions

1 Heat the oil in a frying pan and fry the onion over a moderate heat until softened. Leave to cool, then mix with the pork, chorizo, oregano and seasoning. With floured hands, form into 4 burgers 2–2.5cm/¾–1in thick. Place in a single layer in a shallow dish.

2 Mix the marinade ingredients together in a jug. Pour over the burgers and turn them over so they are evenly coated, then cover and leave in a cool place for 4–8 hours.

3 Lift the burgers from the marinade, reserving it. Cook the burgers in a preheated, oiled griddle pan for 6 minutes on each side, brushing occasionally with the marinade.

4 Meanwhile, toast the halved rolls. Serve the burgers in the rolls with the mayonnaise, lettuce, tomatoes and spring onions.

060 Bacon-Wrapped Sausages with Mustard Dip

PREPARATION TIME 10 minutes, plus 20 minutes soaking the cocktail sticks
COOKING TIME 12–14 minutes   **SERVES** 4–6

12 pork sausages
12 smoked streaky bacon rashers,
  rinds removed
2 tbsp thyme leaves (optional)

MUSTARD DIP
4 tbsp wholegrain mustard
115ml/3¾fl oz/scant ½ cup home-made
  or bought mayonnaise

1 Soak 12 wooden cocktail sticks for 20 minutes. Drain and set aside. Preheat the grill to
  medium-high.Make the mustard dip by beating the mustard into the mayonnaise.
2 Stretch each bacon rasher with the back of a knife. Sprinkle the thyme, if using, over one side
  of each rasher. Place a sausage diagonally across one end of each rasher and roll up to enclose
  the sausage completely, securing the bacon with a cocktail stick.
3 Cook the wrapped sausages on an oiled grill rack under the preheated grill for about 15 minutes
  until well browned and cooked through, turning regularly.

061 Pork & Apple Skewers

PREPARATION TIME 10 minutes, plus 3–4 hours marinating   **COOKING TIME** 12–15 minutes   **SERVES** 4

450g/1lb pork tenderloin, cut into
   3-cm/1¼-in cubes
1 tbsp finely chopped sage leaves
60ml/2fl oz/¼ cup sharp apple juice
juice and finely grated zest of ½ lemon

2 tbsp wholegrain mustard
4 tbsp grapeseed oil
salt and freshly ground black pepper
2 crisp red apples
few sage sprigs

1 Put the pork into a non-metallic bowl.

2 Mix the sage, apple juice, lemon juice and zest, mustard, oil and salt and black pepper together in a jug. Stir into the pork to ensure the cubes are evenly coated, then cover and leave to marinate in a cool place for 3–4 hours.

3 Meanwhile, core the apples and cut into wedges. Preheat the grill to medium-high.

4 Lift the pork from the bowl, reserving the marinade. Thread the pork and apple alternately on to skewers, interspersing the pieces with sage leaves.

5 Cook on an oiled grill rack under the preheated grill for 12–15 minutes, turning regularly and brushing with the remaining marinade, until the pork is cooked through.

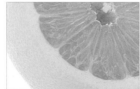

062 Pork Chops with Plum Sauce

PREPARATION TIME 15 minutes   COOKING TIME 30–35 minutes   SERVES 6

6 pork chops, 2.5cm/1in thick
groundnut oil, for brushing
salt and freshly ground black pepper

PLUM SAUCE
1 tbsp groundnut oil
2 shallots, finely chopped

1 tbsp finely chopped fresh root ginger
1½ tsp Sichuan peppercorns, finely crushed
225g/8oz plums, quartered and pitted
1 tbsp light soy sauce
5 tbsp sweet sherry
1½ tsp clear honey
lime juice, to taste

1 Make the plum sauce by heating the oil in a frying pan, adding the shallots and frying until softened. Add the ginger and peppercorns towards the end and continue cooking until they smell fragrant. Add the plums, soy sauce, sherry and honey. Bring to the boil, then reduce the heat and simmer, covered, until the plums are tender. Add lime juice to taste. Set aside.
2 Preheat the oven to 180°C/350°F/Gas 4, or preheat the grill to medium-high.
3 Trim any excess fat from the chops and snip the remaining fat at 2.5-cm/1-in intervals. Brush the chops with oil and season them. Place in an ovenproof dish.
4 Cook the chops in the preheated oven for about 25 minutes, or under the grill for 12-15 minutes until the juices run clear when the thickest part is pierced with a skewer. Meanwhile, warm the sauce in a saucepan over a low heat. Serve the chops with the sauce.

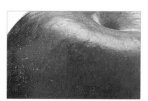

063 Char Sui Pork

PREPARATION TIME 10 minutes, plus 4–6 hours marinating   COOKING TIME 14–16 minutes   SERVES 4

4 pork shoulder steaks

MARINADE
1 tbsp sunflower oil
1 tbsp sesame oil
2 tbsp hoisin sauce
2 tbsp clear honey
2 tbsp soy sauce
1 tsp Chinese five-spice powder
freshly ground black pepper
2 garlic cloves, finely chopped
5-cm/2-in piece fresh root ginger, grated

TO SERVE
6 spring onions, sliced lengthways into
    thin shreds
½ cucumber, deseeded and cut into long,
    thin strips
Chinese plum sauce
lime wedges

1 Lay the pork steaks in a single layer in a shallow non-metallic dish.
2 Make the marinade by stirring together all the ingredients, except the ginger. Using a garlic press, squeeze the ginger juice into the other ingredients, then stir in. Pour over the pork, turn the steaks to ensure they are completely coated, then cover and leave to marinate in a cool place for at least 4–6 hours, turning occasionally. Preheat the grill to medium-high.
3 Lift the pork from the marinade (reserving the remaining marinade) and cook on an oiled grill rack under the preheated grill for 14–16 minutes, turning once and basting with any remaining marinade, until the juices run clear when the thickest part of the steak is pierced with a skewer. Serve the steaks with the spring onions, cucumber, plum sauce and lime wedges.

064 Pizza with Aubergine & Chorizo

PREPARATION TIME 10 minutes, plus rising time and making the sauce   **COOKING TIME** 20–30 minutes
SERVES 4

350g/12oz strong white flour, plus extra for
  rolling the dough
2 tsp easy-blend dried yeast
1 tsp salt
200ml/7fl oz/scant 1 cup warm water
2 tbsp olive oil, plus extra for brushing
1½ recipe quantities Red Pepper & Tomato
  Sauce, omitting the basil (see page 54)
freshly ground black pepper

TOPPING
1 aubergine, sliced
olive oil, for brushing
175g/6oz chorizo, chopped
75g/3oz feta cheese, crumbled
75g/3oz mozzarella cheese, grated
small handful of fresh basil leaves, torn

1 Stir the flour, yeast, salt and some pepper together in a bowl. Make a well in the centre and
  pour in the water and oil, bringing the flour mixture into the liquids to make a soft dough.
  Knead on a floured surface for 10–12 minutes until firm and elastic.
2 Turn the dough over in an oiled bowl, cover and leave to rise until doubled. Preheat the grill to high.
3 Brush the aubergine slices with oil and grill until tender and lightly charred.
4 Preheat the oven to 220°C/425°F/Gas 7. Knock the dough back and divide it in half. Roll each
  piece out on a lightly floured surface to an even 25cm/10in circle. Transfer to two baking sheets.
5 Brush the tops of the pizzas with oil. Spread over the pepper and tomato sauce, leaving a
  1-cm/½-in border. Arrange the aubergine slices over the top, then scatter with the chorizo
  and cheeses. Season with plenty of black pepper and scatter with the basil. Brush the tops
  of the pizzas again with oil.
6 Cook in the preheated oven for 15–20 minutes until the cheese has melted.

065 Sweet & Sticky Spare Ribs

PREPARATION TIME 5 minutes   COOKING TIME 1 hour   SERVES 6

5 garlic cloves, crushed and finely chopped

7.5-cm/3-in piece fresh root ginger, grated

6 tbsp soy sauce

6 tbsp dry sherry

6 tbsp clear honey

2 tsp chilli sauce

1.4kg/3lb meaty pork spare ribs

lemon wedges, to serve

1 Preheat the oven to 200°C/400°F/Gas 6. Combine the garlic, ginger, soy sauce, sherry, honey and chilli sauce in a bowl to make the baste.

2 Lay the ribs in a large foil-lined roasting tin, pour the baste over the top and cook in the preheated oven for 15 minutes, then reduce the temperature to 160°C/325°F/Gas 3 and cook for a further 45 minutes.

3 Remove from the oven and transfer to a board, then divide into individual ribs. Serve with the lemon wedges.

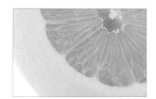

066 Coriander Noodle Salad

PREPARATION TIME 10 minutes   COOKING TIME 10 minutes   SERVES 4

450g/1lb lean boneless pork, cubed

1 garlic clove, finely crushed

olive oil, for frying

225g/8oz dried Chinese egg noodles

6 spring onions, thinly sliced on the
diagonal

1 tbsp soy sauce

2 tbsp Thai fish sauce

1½ tbsp sesame oil

juice and finely grated zest of 1 lime

2 tbsp groundnut oil

2 tbsp sesame seeds, lightly toasted

3 tbsp chopped coriander

2 tbsp chopped fresh root ginger

few drops of chilli oil

freshly ground black pepper

1 Fry the pork and garlic in a little oil in a frying pan over a moderate heat for about 10 minutes, stirring frequently, until lightly browned and cooked through.

2 Meanwhile, cook the noodles in a saucepan of boiling water following the packet instructions. While the pork is cooking, combine the remaining ingredients in a bowl or jug.

3 Drain the noodles into a colander, then tip into a serving bowl with the pork and garlic. Pour the dressing over and toss well to mix.

067 Koftas

PREPARATION TIME 15 minutes, plus at least 4 hours marinating and making the raita
COOKING TIME 10–13 minutes   **SERVES 4**

1 small onion, quartered
2 garlic cloves, chopped
2.5-cm/1-in piece fresh root ginger, chopped
1 tsp ground cumin
1 tsp ground coriander
1 tbsp olive oil, plus extra for brushing
450g/1lb frozen minced lamb, thawed

3 tbsp chopped coriander
1 egg, beaten
salt and freshly ground black pepper
cumin seeds, toasted and crushed,
   for sprinkling
1 recipe quantity Raita (see page 38)
   and some lemon wedges, to serve

1 Put the onion, garlic and ginger in a small blender or food processor and blend until finely
   chopped. Add the spices and mix again until evenly combined.
2 Heat the oil in a frying pan, add the onion mixture and fry for 2–3 minutes, stirring. Leave to cool.
3 Put the lamb into a bowl and break it up with a fork. Add the cold onion mixture, the coriander
   and seasoning, then mix in enough egg to bind, but don't add so much that the mixture becomes
   sticky. Cover and keep in a cool place for up to 4 hours, or overnight in the fridge if possible.
4 Preheat the grill to high. Divide the mixture into 8 equal portions. With wet hands, mould each
   portion into a long sausage around a skewer (soaked if wooden).
5 Brush the koftas with oil and cook on an oiled grill rack under the preheated grill for 8–10 minutes,
   turning occasionally, until nicely browned on the outside and cooked to your liking inside.
6 Sprinkle the koftas with the cumin seeds and serve with the raita and lemon wedges.

068 Butterflied Chinese Lamb

PREPARATION TIME 15 minutes, plus at least 8 hours marinating   COOKING TIME 1 hour 5–10 minutes
SERVES 8

1 butterflied shoulder of lamb, about
1.1kg/2lb 7 oz
4 garlic cloves, cut into thin slivers

MARINADE
150ml/5fl oz/scant ⅔ cup soy sauce
150ml/5fl oz/scant ⅔ cup Madeira or
medium-dry sherry
2.5-cm/1-in piece fresh root ginger, grated
1 tbsp clear honey
3 star anise
3 tbsp chopped coriander
freshly ground black pepper

1 Make the marinade by mixing all the ingredients in a blender.

2 Open out the lamb and cut a few slits all over the surface. Insert the garlic slivers into the
slits. Put the lamb into a baking dish and pour over the marinade. Cover and leave in a cool
place for 8 hours or overnight, turning occasionally. Preheat the oven to 200°C/400°F/Gas 6.

3 Lift the lamb from the marinade (reserving the marinade) and cook in the preheated oven for
1 hour 5–10 minutes, basting occasionally with the remaining marinade, then remove from
the oven, cover and leave to rest for 10 minutes before carving.

069 Baked Rigatoni alla Bolognese

PREPARATION TIME 5 minutes, plus making the sauce and ragù   COOKING TIME 25–30 minutes
SERVES 4–6

450g/1lb rigatoni

6 tbsp freshly grated Parmesan cheese

⅔ recipe quantity Béchamel Sauce
(see page 90)

olive oil, for drizzling

FOR THE RAGÙ

1 large onion, finely chopped

1 carrot, finely chopped

1 small celery stick, finely chopped

olive oil, for frying

2 garlic cloves, finely chopped

450g/1lb minced beef

325ml/11fl oz/scant 1⅓ cups red wine

325ml/11fl oz/scant 1⅓ cups beef stock

400g/14oz/1⅔ cups tinned chopped
tomatoes

1 tbsp sun-dried tomato paste

2 tsp dried oregano

salt and freshly ground black pepper

1 Preheat the oven to 200°C/400°F/Gas 6.

2 To make the ragu sauce, fry the onion, carrot and celery in a little oil in a heavy-based pan until softened. Add the garlic and cook for 1 minute, then stir in the beef and cook, stirring, until lightly browned. Stir in the remaining ingredients and bring to the boil, then reduce the heat and simmer, half-covered, stirring occasionally, for about 40 minutes, until the sauce has reduced.

3 Meanwhile, cook the rigatoni in a large saucepan of boiling water following the packet instructions, but for 2 minutes less than suggested, and drain well. Toss the pasta with 4 tbsp of the Parmesan, then the ragù and béchamel sauce. When well mixed, spread evenly in a gratin dish, sprinkle over the remaining Parmesan and drizzle with a little oil.

4 Bake for 15–20 minutes until browned. Leave to stand for 5 minutes before serving

070 Lasagne alla Bolognese

PREPARATION TIME 15 minutes, plus making the ragù and 30 minutes infusing
COOKING TIME 45 minutes   **SERVES** 6

12 lasagne sheets

olive oil, for cooking the pasta and oiling

1 recipe quantity Ragù (see page 88)

3 tbsp freshly grated Parmesan cheese

BÉCHAMEL SAUCE

750ml/26fl oz/3 cups milk

1 bay leaf

1 onion slice

1 clove

75g/2½oz butter

6 tbsp plain flour

1 Preheat the oven to 200°C/400°F/Gas 6.

2 Cook the lasagne sheets in batches in boiling salted water, to which a little oil has been added, for 3 minutes for fresh lasagne or 7 minutes for dried. Drain the lasagne, then rinse it and drain again. Spread on a clean tea towel to dry. (Follow these instructions even if using no-pre-cook lasagne.)

3 To make the béchamel sauce, gently heat the milk with the bay leaf, onion slice and clove, then remove from the heat, cover and leave to infuse for 30 minutes. Melt the butter over a low heat in a heavy-based saucepan, then stir in the flour and mix to a paste. Cook for 1–2 minutes. Remove the pan from the heat and slowly strain in the milk, whisking or stirring continually to prevent lumps forming. Once all the milk has been incorporated, return the pan to the heat and just bring to the boil, then simmer for 5 minutes, stirring occasionally. Season.

4 Spread a thin layer of béchamel over the bottom of an oiled ovenproof dish (about 30 x 20 x 7.5cm/ 12 x 8 x 3in). Add a layer of 4 lasagne sheets, then one of ragù. Add another layer of béchamel, followed by a layer of lasagne. Repeat the layering to make 3 layers of pasta, 3 of ragù and 4 of béchamel. Sprinkle the Parmesan over the top layer of béchamel.

5 Bake in the preheated oven for about 25 minutes until the top is crisp and golden and the lasagne heated throughout. Allow to stand for 5 minutes before serving.

071 Beef & Mushroom Burgers

PREPARATION TIME 15 minutes, plus 20 minutes soaking   **COOKING TIME** 13–15 minutes   **SERVES** 4

2 tbsp dried mushrooms
small knob of unsalted butter
150g/5oz mushrooms, chopped
1 garlic clove, finely chopped
450g/1lb minced beef
4 tsp wholegrain mustard
2 tbsp chopped herbs (marjoram, tarragon,
   parsley, sage or thyme)
salt and freshly ground black pepper

4 hamburger buns or rolls, split horizontally,
   and salad leaves, to serve

ROASTED RED PEPPER DRESSING
1 red pepper, halved and deseeded
2 tbsp balsamic vinegar
1 tsp thyme
1 tsp chopped garlic
6 tbsp olive oil

1 Place the dried mushrooms in a bowl and just cover with boiling water. Soak for 20 minutes,
   then drain, pat dry and chop finely.
2 Melt the butter in a frying pan, add the fresh mushrooms and garlic and fry until the liquid has
   been given off and the mushrooms are tender. Stir in the soaked mushrooms just before the
   end of cooking. Leave to cool.
3 Mix the beef with the mushroom mixture, mustard, herbs and seasoning until thoroughly
   combined. Divide the mixture into 4 equal portions. With wet hands, form each portion into
   a patty approximately 2.5cm/1in thick.
4 To make the dressing, grill the red pepper and remove the skin (see page 83). Put into a
   blender with the vinegar, thyme and garlic. Pulse to mix, then, with the motor running, slowly
   pour in the olive oil until smooth. Season to taste.
5 Cook the burgers in a preheated, oiled griddle pan for 4–5 minutes on each side for medium-rare,
   or for longer if you prefer them more well done, turning them carefully.
6 Toast the rolls. Mix the salad leaves with a little dressing, then put them on the bottom of each roll.
   Top with the burgers and spoon a little dressing over. Cover with the tops of the rolls and serve.

Chapter 4

VEGETARIAN

Dishes that do not contain meat, poultry or fish are usually cheaper than those that do, but that does not mean that eating vegetarian meals is less fun or interesting; in fact, I think the opposite is true.

To keep costs down, you can buy dried beans and lentils rather than canned. The varieties on sale now cook more quickly than their cousins of yesteryear, with even chickpeas cooking in about 1 hour. Soaking cuts down the cooking time (to speed the soaking, boil the beans for 10 minutes, cover and then leave to soak for just a couple of hours, or longer if you wish).

Cheese is used quite often in vegetarian cooking. Buy a mature cheese with a good flavour, rather than a cheap mild one, otherwise you'll just use more. And make the most of herbs and spices to create stunning meals.

Gnocchi alla Romana (see page 94)

072 Gnocchi alla Romana

PREPARATION TIME 5 minutes, plus 2 hours chilling   **COOKING TIME** 25–30 minutes   **SERVES** 4

2 cloves

2 onions

1 litre/35fl oz/4 cups milk

2 bay leaves

175g/6oz/scant 1½ cups semolina

2 egg yolks

75g/2½oz Parmesan cheese, freshly grated

115g/4oz unsalted butter, melted

1 tbsp Dijon mustard

salt and freshly ground black pepper

crisp green salad, to serve

1 Stick the cloves into the onions. Pour the milk into a heavy-based saucepan and add the onions and bay leaves. Bring to the boil slowly, then remove from the heat, cover and leave to infuse for 10 minutes. Strain the milk and return to the rinsed pan. Bring to the boil. Over a medium heat, gradually whisk in the semolina in a thin, steady stream. Return to the boil, then reduce the heat and simmer for 3–5 minutes until thick and smooth, stirring constantly.

2 Off the heat, gradually beat in the egg yolks, then add two-thirds of the Parmesan, half the butter and the mustard. Season, using plenty of black pepper. Using a dampened palette knife or back of a spoon, spread the mixture in a layer approximately 1cm/½in thick on a moistened baking sheet. Brush with the remaining butter. Cool and then chill for about 2 hours until firm.

3 Preheat the oven to 230°C/450°F/Gas 8.

4 Cut the gnocchi into 5-cm/2-in rounds with a plain biscuit cutter. Arrange in a buttered gratin dish or individual dishes and sprinkle with the remaining Parmesan. Bake in the preheated oven for 15–20 minutes until heated and browned. Serve accompanied by a crisp green salad.

073 Tagliatelle with Green Beans & Herbs

PREPARATION TIME 10 minutes   COOKING TIME 15 minutes   SERVES 4

350g/12oz mixed frozen runner beans,
French beans and peas
400g/14oz tagliatelle
1 garlic clove, crushed
olive oil, for frying
150g/5oz soft, mild goats' cheese, chopped
small bunch of flat-leaf parsley,
finely chopped

leaves from a small bunch of young mint,
finely chopped
100ml/3½fl oz/scant ½ cup crème fraîche
salt and freshly ground black pepper
2 tbsp lightly toasted pine nuts and some
shaved pecorino cheese, to serve

1 Bring a large saucepan of water to the boil, add the beans and peas and cook for 3–4 minutes until almost tender. Remove with a slotted spoon and set aside. Bring the water back to the boil, add the pasta to the pan and cook according to the packet instructions until just cooked or al dente.

2 Meanwhile, fry the garlic in a little oil in a frying pan over a low heat for about 2 minutes. Add the goats' cheese, herbs and crème fraîche. Slice the runner beans thinly lengthways and the French beans in half widthways and add to the mixture. Warm through and season.

3 Drain the pasta and toss with the sauce. Serve scattered with the pine nuts and pecorino.

074 **Pasta with Courgettes, Lemon & Pine Nuts**

PREPARATION TIME 10 minutes   **COOKING TIME** 10 minutes   **SERVES** 4

350g/12oz pasta, such as torchieti or fusilli

2 plump garlic cloves, thinly sliced

4 tbsp virgin olive oil

550g/1lb 4oz small courgettes, pared into ribbons using a vegetable peeler

juice and finely grated zest of 1 large lemon

75ml/2½fl oz/scant ⅓ cup double cream

2 tbsp finely chopped flat-leaf parsley

5 tbsp pine nuts, lightly toasted

salt and freshly ground black pepper

freshly grated Parmesan cheese, to sprinkle

1 Cook the pasta in a large saucepan of boiling water following the packet instructions until just cooked or al dente.

2 Meanwhile, put the garlic and oil in a small saucepan and warm for 5 minutes. Do not let the oil boil or the garlic will fry. Discard the garlic.

3 Pour the garlic-infused oil into a frying pan and fry the courgettes briskly in batches until golden. Return all the courgettes to the pan with the lemon juice and zest and the cream. Bubble for 2–3 minutes until thickened slightly, then season.

4 Drain the pasta, add to the courgette sauce with the parsley and pine nuts and toss together. Sprinkle with Parmesan before serving.

075 Pappardelle with Squash & Goats' Cheese

PREPARATION TIME 10 minutes   COOKING TIME 30 minutes   SERVES 4

1 small butternut squash, peeled, deseeded
  and cut into 2.5-cm/1in-chunks
several thyme sprigs
2 garlic cloves, crushed
3 tbsp olive oil
300g/10½oz pappardelle

4 slices goats' cheese log
4 tbsp finely chopped flat-leaf parsley
finely grated zest of ½ lemon
extra-virgin olive oil, to drizzle
freshly grated Parmesan cheese, to scatter
salt and freshly ground black pepper

1 Preheat the oven to 200°C/400°F/Gas 6.
2 Put the squash into a large roasting tin, add the thyme, garlic and oil and stir together to coat
   the squash. Roast in the preheated oven for 25–30 minutes until the squash is tender and
   tinged with brown. Discard the thyme.
3 Meanwhile, cook the pasta in a large saucepan of boiling water following the packet instructions
   until just cooked or al dente and drain well, reserving 125ml/4fl oz/½ cup of the cooking water.
4 Lay the goats' cheese slices on a piece of lightly oiled foil and grill for 3–4 minutes until lightly
   browned and softened.
5 Toss the pasta with the squash and any pan juices, the parsley, lemon zest and seasoning,
   adding enough of the reserved cooking water to moisten. Drizzle with extra-virgin olive oil and
   scatter with Parmesan, then place the goats' cheese on top and serve.

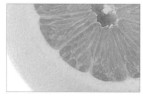

076 Risotto with Minted Lettuce & Peas

PREPARATION TIME 5 minutes   COOKING TIME 30 minutes   SERVES 4

1 onion, finely chopped
40g/1½oz/3 tbsp unsalted butter
300g/10oz/1⅓ cups risotto rice
150ml/5fl oz/scant ⅔ cup medium-bodied
  dry white wine
875ml/30 fl oz/3½ cups boiling
  vegetable stock

225g/8oz/1½ cups frozen peas
175g/6oz Little Gem lettuce,
  shredded
2 tbsp chopped mint
4 tbsp crème fraîche (optional)
squeeze of lemon juice (optional)
salt and freshly ground black pepper

1 Fry the onion in the butter in a large frying pan over a moderate heat until softened. Add the
rice and stir for 2–3 minutes until all the grains are coated with the butter.

2 Add the wine and cook gently, stirring occasionally, until the rice has absorbed almost all the
liquid, then add the hot stock, a ladleful at a time, in the same way until the rice is thick and
creamy and just tender. Add the peas 5 minutes before the end of the cooking time

3 Stir in the lettuce, mint and seasoning. Serve the risotto with a spoonful of crème fraîche stirred
into each portion or add a squeeze of lemon juice.

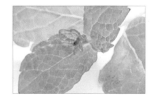

077 Pearl Barley with Mushrooms & Leeks

PREPARATION TIME 5 minutes   COOKING TIME 45 minutes   SERVES 4

olive oil, for frying
100g/3½oz shiitake mushrooms, sliced
200g/7oz mushrooms, sliced
2 leeks, sliced
3 garlic cloves, crushed
225g/8oz/1 cup pearl barley

1.25l/40fl oz/4¾ cups vegetable stock
leaves from a small bunch of flat-leaf
   parsley, finely chopped
salt and freshly ground black pepper
freshly grated Parmesan cheese, to sprinkle
   (optional)

1 Heat the oil in a large frying pan and fry both types of mushrooms and the leeks over
   a moderate heat until golden, adding the garlic and pearl barley towards the end.
2 Add the vegetable stock and bring to the boil, then reduce the heat and simmer, half-covered,
   for about 40 minutes until the barley is tender and all the liquid has been absorbed (adding
   a little extra stock or some water if necessary). Season and add the parsley. Sprinkle with
   Parmesan, if desired, and serve.

078 Spinach & Cheese Lasagne

PREPARATION TIME 15 minutes, plus making the sauce   COOKING TIME 45 minutes   SERVES 6

12 lasagne sheets
olive oil, for cooking the lasagne and oiling
900g/2lb spinach, rinsed
small knob of unsalted butter
225g/8oz/scant 1 cup ricotta cheese
175g/6oz Gorgonzola cheese, crumbled

1 recipe quantity Béchamel Sauce
  (see page 90)
4 tbsp pine nuts, lightly toasted
50g/1¾oz Parmesan cheese, freshly grated
200g/7oz buffalo mozzarella cheese, grated
salt and freshly ground black pepper

1 Cook the lasagne sheets in batches in boiling salted water, to which a little oil has been added, for 3 minutes for fresh lasagne or 7 minutes for dried. Drain the lasagne, then rinse it and drain again. Spread on a clean tea towel to dry. (Follow these instructions even if using no-pre-cook lasagne.)

2 Preheat the oven to 180°C/350°F/Gas 4.

3 Cook the spinach in a large saucepan, with just the water clinging to its leaves. Stirring frequently, until wilted and soft. Drain, chop coarsely and then squeeze out as much water as possible. Combine with the butter, ricotta, Gorgonzola and seasoning.

4 Barely cover the base of an oiled ovenproof dish (25 x 16 x 7.5cm/10 x 6¼ x 3in) with some of the béchamel sauce. Cover with 3 of the lasagne sheets, then a quarter of the spinach mixture and scatter over 1 tablespoon of the pine nuts. Pour over a third of the remaining béchamel and sprinkle a quarter of the Parmesan on top. Repeat the layers, adding a third of the mozzarella with the pine nuts until the ingredients are used up, ending with mozzarella and Parmesan.

5 Bake in the preheated oven for 30–35 minutes until bubbling and golden. Leave to stand for 5 minutes before serving.

079 Courgette & Ricotta Cannelloni

PREPARATION TIME 15 minutes, plus making the sauce   **COOKING TIME** 25 minutes   **SERVES** 4

12 lasagne verde sheets
olive oil, for cooking the lasagne,
   frying and oiling
1 onion, chopped
4 courgettes, grated
2 garlic cloves, squashed and
   finely chopped

finely grated zest of 1 lemon
250g/9oz/1 cup ricotta cheese
salt and freshly ground black pepper
1 recipe quantity Red Pepper & Tomato
   Sauce (see page 54)
50g/1¾oz Parmesan cheese, freshly grated

1 Cook the lasagne sheets in batches in boiling salted water, to which a little oil has been added, for 3 minutes for fresh lasagne or 7 minutes for dried. Drain the lasagne, then rinse it and drain again. Spread on a clean tea towel to dry. (Follow these instructions even if using no-pre-cook lasagne.)

2 Preheat the oven to 200°C/400°F/Gas 6.

3 Fry the onion in a little oil until softened but not coloured. Stir in the courgettes and garlic and continue cooking, stirring frequently, until softened. Remove from the heat and add the lemon zest, half the ricotta and some seasoning.

4 Spread the courgette mixture down the centre of each lasagne sheet. Roll into tubes.

5 Pour half the sauce into an oiled large, shallow ovenproof dish. Place the tubes on top, seam-side down. Pour over the remaining sauce, dot with the remaining ricotta and sprinkle with Parmesan.

6 Bake in the preheated oven for 15 minutes until golden. Allow to stand for 5 minutes before serving.

080 Souffléed Macaroni Cheese

PREPARATION TIME 10 minutes   COOKING TIME 25–30 minutes   SERVES 4

350g/12oz/2¼ cups macaroni
50g/1¾oz unsalted butter
1 leek, finely chopped
50g/1¾oz/scant ½ cup plain flour
570ml/20fl oz/scant 2⅓ cups milk
1 bay leaf, torn across

175g/6oz/scant ¾ cup ricotta cheese
115g/4oz Fontina cheese, grated
115g/4oz Parmesan cheese, freshly grated
4 eggs, separated
salt and freshly ground black pepper

1 Preheat the oven to 190°C/375°F/Gas 5.

2 Cook the macaroni in a large saucepan of boiling water following the packet instructions, but for 1 minute less than suggested, and drain well.

3 Meanwhile, melt the butter in a heavy-based saucepan and fry the leek over a moderate heat until softened, then stir in the flour for 1 minute. Gradually add the milk and bay leaf, stirring constantly, and bring to the boil, then simmer for 5 minutes, stirring occasionally. Discard the bay leaf. Off the heat, stir in the ricotta, Fontina, half the Parmesan, the egg yolks and macaroni. Season.

4 Whisk the egg whites until soft peaks form. Stir a few spoonfuls into the sauce, then carefully fold in the remainder in 3 batches using a large metal spoon.

5 Transfer the mixture into a large, shallow ovenproof dish, scatter over the remaining Parmesan and bake in the preheated oven for 15–20 minutes until puffed, golden and just set in the centre.

081 Mediterranean Vegetable Tart

PREPARATION TIME 25 minutes, plus at least 30 minutes chilling **COOKING TIME** 50–55 minutes
SERVES 4

1 aubergine, about 300g/10½oz, sliced
olive oil, for frying
175g/6oz mushrooms, sliced
1 large red pepper, thinly sliced
1 onion, thinly sliced
4 large well-flavoured plum tomatoes,
   chopped

2 garlic cloves, chopped
1½ tbsp chopped oregano
salt and freshly ground black pepper

PASTRY
225g/8oz plain flour, plus extra for dusting
115g/4oz chilled butter, diced

1 To make the pastry, sift the flour and a little salt and pepper into a mixing bowl. Add the butter and
rub it into the flour with your fingertips until the mixture resembles breadcrumbs. Sprinkle 3–4
tablespoons of iced water over the surface, then quickly and lightly, using a round-bladed knife,
stir the ingredients together until they form large lumps. With one hand, quickly bring the dough
into a ball. Knead lightly and briefly, then wrap in clingfilm and chill for at least 30 minutes.

2 Meanwhile, stir-fry the aubergine in a little oil in a large deep frying pan until browned. Remove
with a slotted spoon and drain on kitchen paper. Add the mushrooms to the pan and fry until
lightly softened, then remove with a slotted spoon. Repeat with the pepper and the onion. Return
the vegetables to the pan, stir in the tomatoes, garlic, oregano and seasoning and cook for 15
minutes, stirring occasionally, until tender and thickened. Preheat the oven to 200°C/400°F/Gas 6.

3 Meanwhile, roll out the chilled pastry on a floured work surface into a circle large enough to line
a deep 27cm/10¾in flan tin. Lift the pastry into the tin. Prick the base, cover with greaseproof
paper and fill with baking beans, then bake blind in the preheated oven for 15 minutes. Remove
the baking beans and paper and bake for a further 5 minutes until lightly browned and cooked
through. Fill the flan with the vegetable mixture and return to the oven for 5 minutes to heat
through, then serve. Alternatively, leave to cool and serve cold.

082 Vegetable Satay

PREPARATION TIME 15 minutes   COOKING TIME 20 minutes   SERVES 4

1 small squash, peeled and cut into chunks

2 leeks, cut into chunks

1 courgette, cut into chunks

100g/3½oz mushrooms, halved

3 tbsp dark soy sauce

2 tsp sesame oil

8–12 bay leaves

SATAY SAUCE

1 tbsp groundnut oil

1 shallot, finely chopped

2 garlic cloves, crushed

2.5-cm/1-in piece fresh root ginger, grated

1 lemon grass stalk

1 red chilli, deseeded and finely chopped

1 tsp curry powder

150g/5½oz crunchy peanut butter

3 tbsp chopped coriander

a little caster sugar

salt and freshly ground black pepper

1 To make the sauce, heat the oil and fry the shallot, garlic, ginger and lemon grass until softened. Stir in the chilli and curry powder for a couple of minutes, then stir in the peanut butter and 250ml/9fl oz/1 cup boiling water. Bring to the boil, add the coriander and season with a little sugar and salt and pepper to taste. Remove from the heat.

2 Meanwhile, preheat the grill to high. Cook the squash in a pan of boiling water for 5 minutes. Add the leeks and cook for a further 3 minutes. Drain and cool under running cold water. Put into a bowl with the courgette and mushrooms.

3 Combine the soy sauce, sesame oil and some black pepper. Trickle over the vegetables and stir gently to coat all the vegetables.

4 Thread the vegetables alternately on to skewers, adding bay leaves along the way. Cook on an oiled grill rack under the preheated grill for about 8 minutes, turning occasionally.

5 Warm the satay sauce through and serve with the vegetables.

083 Feta-Stuffed Onions

PREPARATION TIME 15 minutes   **COOKING TIME** 35 minutes   **SERVES** 4

4 large onions, about 300g/10½oz each
small knob of unsalted butter
1 large leek, chopped
leaves from 4 thyme sprigs
2 tbsp chopped parsley
115g/4oz feta cheese, crumbled

8 sun-dried tomato halves in oil,
   drained and sliced
6 oil-cured black olives, pitted and chopped
2 egg yolks
freshly ground black pepper

1 Trim the root ends of the onions, but do not cut them off completely because they hold the
  layers together. Cut each onion in half from top to bottom. Remove the inner layers of each
  onion half, leaving a shell 2 layers thick. Chop the removed layers.
2 Add the onion shells to a saucepan of boiling water, then reduce the heat and simmer for
  10 minutes. Lift the onions from the water with a slotted spoon and leave upside-down to
  drain. Preheat the oven to 180°C/350°F/Gas 4.
3 Meanwhile, melt the butter in a heavy-based frying pan. Add the chopped onion and cook over
  a very low heat until very soft and golden. Add the leek about three-quarters of the way
  through. Stir in the thyme and parsley and leave to cool slightly, then add the feta, sun-dried
  tomatoes, olives and egg yolks. Season with plenty of black pepper.
4 Place each onion shell upright in an oiled ovenproof dish and pile the filling into the shells.
  Cover with foil, then bake in the preheated oven for 25 minutes. Serve hot.

084 Roasted Vegetables

PREPARATION TIME 15 minutes, plus 2 hours marinating   COOKING TIME 65 minutes   SERVES 4

900g/2lb mixed vegetables, such as carrots,
  parsnips, courgettes, aubergines, chicory,
  fennel bulb, red onion, small leeks
8 garlic cloves
4 rosemary sprigs
5 tbsp virgin olive oil
1½ tsp balsamic vinegar
salt and freshly ground black pepper

MUSTARD & CAPER SAUCE
175ml/6fl oz/¾ cup home-made or
  bought mayonnaise
1½ tsp Dijon mustard
1½ tsp capers, drained and chopped
3 tbsp chopped flat-leaf parsley

1 Blanch the carrots and parsnips separately in boiling water for 5 minutes, then drain and dry well.

2 Slice the courgettes and aubergines diagonally. Quarter the chicory lengthways and remove the core, but leave the leaves attached. Cut the fennel lengthways into wedges. Cut the red onion into wedges, leaving them attached at the root end, and halve the leeks lengthways.

3 Place all the vegetables and the garlic in a large baking tin and add the rosemary, olive oil, balsamic vinegar and seasoning. Stir everything together, then cover with foil and leave to marinate in a cool place for 2 hours. Preheat the oven to 200°C/400°F/Gas 6.

4 Meanwhile, make the sauce by stirring the ingredients together. Set aside.

5 Cook the vegetables in the preheated oven for 30 minutes, then remove the foil and cook for a further 30 minutes, stirring occastionally, until they are tender and lightly charred. Remove from the oven and serve with the sauce.

085 Vegetable Fajitas

PREPARATION TIME 10 minutes, plus 4 hours marinating   COOKING TIME 30 minutes   SERVES 8

2 red and 2 yellow peppers, quartered
3 courgettes, sliced diagonally
2 aubergines, sliced diagonally
175g/6oz baby corn, halved lengthways
3 mild red chillies
6 tbsp olive oil
2 tbsp chopped mixed parsley, oregano
   and thyme
juice of 1 lime
freshly ground black pepper
16 soft flour tortillas
soured cream, coriander springs and lime
   wedges, to serve

AVOCADO & TOMATO RELISH
1 large avocado, pitted and finely chopped
3 tbsp lime juice
½ red chilli, deseeded and finely chopped
1 vine-ripened plum tomato, deseeded
   and diced
½ red onion, finely diced
handful coriander leaves, chopped

1 Put all the vegetables, including the chillies, into a large bowl. Mix together the olive oil, herbs, lime juice and black pepper to taste and stir into the vegetables, then cover and leave to marinate for about 4 hours, stirring occasionally.

2 Meanwhile, make the relish by tossing the ingredients together. Cover and chill for 30 minutes.

3 Lift the vegetables from the marinade and cook in batches in a preheated oiled griddle pan until softened and lightly charred. Remove the vegetables that are cooked first as soon as they are ready, put into a bowl and cover with clingfilm.

4 Meanwhile, warm the tortillas following the packet instructions.

5 When the chillies are cool enough to handle, cut off the tops. Chop them, discarding the seeds.

6 Divide the vegetables and chillies among the tortillas. Top with avocado relish, spoon on some soured cream and fold over. Serve with coriander springs and lime wedges.

086 Spiced Lentil Burgers

PREPARATION TIME 15 minutes, plus making the relish and at least 1 hour chilling
COOKING TIME 40 minutes–1 hour   **SERVES** 4

225g/8oz/scant 1¼ cups green or brown
   lentils
3 tbsp olive oil
2 large onions, finely chopped
2 carrots, finely chopped
1 celery stick, finely chopped
2 garlic cloves, finely chopped
1 tsp ground cumin

1 tsp ground coriander
3 tbsp chopped parsley
3 tbsp chopped coriander
1 tbsp lemon juice
salt and freshly ground black pepper
seasoned plain flour, for coating
1 recipe quantity Yogurt & Mint Relish
   (see page 111)

1 Cook the lentils in boiling unsalted water for 20–30 minutes until tender. Drain well and leave
to cool.

2 Meanwhile, heat 1 tablespoon of the olive oil in a large frying pan and fry the onions, carrots
and celery over a moderate heat for 10 minutes until softened and lightly browned. Stir in the
lentils, garlic, spices, herbs, lemon juice and seasoning. Scrape into a food processor or blender
and blend to a coarse purée that holds together; alternatively, mash with a potato masher.

3 With floured hands, form the mixture into 12 burgers about 1–2cm/½–¾in thick. Coat the
burgers in seasoned flour and pat in gently. Cover and chill for at least 1 hour to firm up,
or overnight, if possible, to allow the flavours to develop.

4 Heat 1 tablespoon of the oil in the frying pan and cook the burgers in batches for 5–7 minutes
on each side until crisp and browned. Remove with a fish slice and leave to each batch drain
on kitchen paper in a warm place while you cook the remaining burgers in the remaining oil.
Serve with the avocado and tomato relish.

087 Falafel Burgers with Yogurt & Mint Relish

PREPARATION TIME 10 minutes, plus 2 hours chilling   COOKING TIME 10–20 minutes   SERVES 4

800g/1lb 12oz tinned chickpeas, drained
 and rinsed
1 garlic clove, chopped
2 tbsp tahini
1 tsp ground cumin
1 tsp ground coriander
50g/³⁄₄oz/scant ²⁄₃ cup fresh breadcrumbs
3 tbsp chopped coriander
seasoned plain flour, for dusting
salt and freshly ground black pepper
pitta bread and lettuce leaves, to serve

YOGURT & MINT RELISH
1 small garlic clove, peeled
150ml/5fl oz/scant ²⁄₃ cup Greek yogurt
4 tbsp chopped mint, plus small spring of
 mint leaves, to garnish
dash of Tabasco sauce

1 Put all the burger ingredients except the flour into a food processor and mix until the chickpeas are finely chopped, but do not let the mixture turn into a purée.

2 Transfer to a bowl and stir in about 2 tablespoons of water, kneading until the mixture holds together. With well-floured hands, form the mixture into 8 burgers about 2.5cm/1in thick. Chill for at least 2 hours. Preheat the grill to high.

3 To make the relish, crush the garlic with a pinch of salt, then mix it with the yogurt. Add the mint and season with Tabasco and black pepper, to taste. Chill before serving. Garnish with the mint leaves to serve.

4 Cook the burgers on an oiled grill rack under the preheated grill for about 5 minutes on each side (in batches if necessary) until crisp and brown on the outside and warmed through.

5 Meanwhile, warm the pitta breads in a microwave oven or toaster. Split the pitta breads open, add the falafel and top with the lettuce. Serve with the yogurt and mint relish.

088 Leek & Goats' Cheese Sausages

PREPARATION TIME 20 minutes, plus 4½ hours chilling   **COOKING TIME** 20–25 minutes   **SERVES** 4

300g/10½oz potatoes, chopped
75g/2½oz soft goats' cheese
15g/½oz butter, plus extra for greasing
125g/4½oz leeks, finely chopped
50g/¾oz feta cheese, crumbled

25g/1oz/⅓ cup fresh breadcrumbs,
   plus extra for coating
salt and freshly ground black pepper
1–2 eggs (as needed), beaten
salad leaves and mayonnaise, to serve

1 Cook the potatoes in boiling salted water for 10–15 minutes or until tender, then drain well. Return to the pan over a low heat and shake the pan gently to dry the potatoes. Remove from the heat. Mash the potatoes and beat in the goats' cheese. Set aside.

2 Melt the butter in a frying pan and fry the leeks over a low heat until very soft and dry. Beat them into the potato with the feta, breadcrumbs and seasoning, using plenty of black pepper. Transfer to a plate, cover and chill for at least 4 hours.

3 With floured hands, shape the mixture into 8 sausages. Put the beaten egg(s) in a bowl and the extra breadcrumbs on a plate. Dip the sausages in the beaten egg, then roll them in the breadcrumbs until they are evenly coated, pressing the crumbs in lightly. Cover with cling film and chill for 30 minutes. Preheat the grill to high.

4 Cook on an greased grill rack under the grill for about 3 minutes until browned and crisp, then turn over and cook on the other side. Serve with a green salad and mayonnaise, if desired.

089 Courgette Burgers with Dill Tzatziki

PREPARATION TIME 15 minutes, plus 1½–2 hours degorging and chilling
COOKING TIME 15–20 minutes **SERVES** 4

500g/1lb 2oz small courgettes, grated
175g/6oz/2¼ cups fresh breadcrumbs
2 eggs, lightly beaten
6 spring onions, very finely chopped
1 heaped tbsp chopped mint
2 heaped tbsp chopped parsley
flour, for dusting

salt and freshly ground black pepper
olive oil, for frying
4 ciabatta rolls, split into halves

DILL TZATZIKI
400ml/14fl oz/1⅔ cups Greek-style yogurt
2 tbsp chopped dill

1 Layer the courgettes and a good sprinkling of salt in a colander. Leave for 30–60 minutes.

2 Meanwhile, preheat the oven to 190°C/375°F/Gas 5. Reserve 4 tablespoons of the breadcrumbs and spread the remainder on a baking sheet. Bake for 10 minutes, stirring occasionally, until brown and crisp. Remove from the oven, spread on a plate and set aside to cool.

3 Rinse the courgettes thoroughly and squeeze firmly to expel as much water as possible, then pat dry between 2 clean tea towels.

4 Mix the courgettes with the reserved breadcrumbs, the eggs, spring onions, herbs and some black pepper. With floured hands, form into 16 burgers about 1–2cm/½–¾in thick. Coat evenly and thoroughly in the toasted breadcrumbs, pressing them in. Leave, uncovered, in the fridge for 1 hour.

5 Make the tzatziki by beating the yogurt until smooth, then stir in the dill and season.

6 Heat a little oil in a large frying pan and fry the burgers in batches for 3–4 minutes until browned and crisp underneath, then turn carefully and cook on the other side.

7 Meanwhile, lightly toast the rolls. Serve the burgers in the rolls with the tzatziki spooned on top.

090 Tofu Kebabs

PREPARATION TIME 15 minutes, plus at least 4 hours marinating   **COOKING TIME** 20–30 minutes
SERVES 4

250g/9oz firm tofu, drained and cut into
 2.5-cm/1-in cubes
8 baby onions, peeled
1 large yellow pepper
8 cherry tomatoes, preferably plum

TOFU MARINADE
1 tbsp dark soy sauce
1 tbsp dry sherry
1 tbsp sesame oil

1 tsp Dijon mustard
1 large garlic clove, finely chopped
2 tsp rice wine vinegar

KEBAB MARINADE
1 tbsp sherry vinegar
1½ tsp Dijon vinegar
1 small garlic clove, finely chopped
5 tbsp olive oil
1½ tsp finely chopped mixed herbs

1 Make the tofu marinade by combining the ingredients. Add the tofu and turn the cubes over
  to make sure they are evenly coated. Cover and leave in a cool place for at least 4 hours,
  preferably overnight.

2 Preheat the grill to high. Blanch the onions in boiling water for 2–3 minutes, drain and refresh
  under cold running water. Drain again and leave to drain further on kitchen paper.

3 Cook the yellow pepper in a grill pan under the preheated grill for 10–15 minutes until charred
  and blistered. Leave until cool enough to handle, then peel off the skin and slice the flesh into
  8 strips.

4 Make the kebab marinade by shaking the ingredients together in a screw-topped jar. Season.

5 Lift the tofu from the marinade and thread alternately on to skewers (soaked if wooden)
  with the vegetables. Brush with the kebab marinade.

6 Cook on an oiled grill rack under the preheated grill for about 8 minutes, turning regularly,
  until browned.

091 Ratatouille Pie

PREPARATION TIME 10 minutes, plus 1 hour degorging and making the pastry
COOKING TIME 1 hour 10–20 minutes   **SERVES** 4–6

1 aubergine, sliced
olive oil, for frying
1 large red pepper, sliced
3 small courgettes, quite thickly sliced
1 large onion, thinly sliced
3 garlic cloves, crushed and chopped

2 large, ripe tomatoes, chopped
a few sprigs of thyme, marjoram and parsley
leaves from a few sprigs of basil, shredded
1½ recipe quantities pastry (see page 104)
salt and freshly ground black pepper

1 Sprinkle the aubergine slices with salt and leave in a colander to drain for 1 hour. Rinse them thoroughly, then dry well.

2 Heat a little oil in a large frying pan, add the aubergine slices, in batches if necessary, and fry until lightly browned. Remove with a fish slice and drain on kitchen paper. Add the pepper to the pan and fry for a few minutes until softened, but take care not to overcook it, then remove as before. Finally, cook the courgettes in a little more oil, if needed, until just beginning to soften, stirring occasionally, then remove.

3 Fry the onion, adding a little more oil if necessary, and cook until softened, stirring frequently. Stir in the garlic and tomatoes for a few minutes, then return the other vegetables to the pan and add the thyme, marjoram and parsley. Season lightly, and add 2 tablespoons of oil, if desired. Cover and cook gently for 30–35 minutes, stirring occasionally. Stir in the basil, remove from the heat and leave to cool, uncovered. Preheat the oven to 200°C/400°F/Gas 6.

4 Roll out two-thirds of the chilled pasty and use to line a deep 25cm/10in flan tin. Bake blind for 15 minutes (see page 104), then remove from the oven and remove the paper and beans.

5 Roll out the remaining pastry to make a lid for the pie. Fill the pastry case with the cold vegetable mixture, carefully put the lid in place and press the edges together. Cut a small slit in the lid. Return to the oven and bake for 15–20 minutes until browned. Serve warm or cold.

Chapter 5

DESSERTS

My favourite desserts are fruit-based. These don't cost much because you can buy fruit that is part of a special promotion and/or in season. If you go to farm shops or pick-your-own farms you can buy larger amounts cheaply and then preserve the surplus in some way, usually freezing. Many apples can be kept just as they are, in a cool, dry place, and they will last for ages.

Out-of-season, frozen mixed fruits, such as fruits of the forest fruits, are better value than their fresh counterparts, and for many uses, such as the recipe shown here, work just as well. Canned fruits in natural juice are also useful. Many fruit puddings require very little or no cooking, but if you fancy a traditional baked pudding, one of my top choices is a Queen of Puddings (see page 127), which is quick, easy and economical.

Summer Berry Parcels (see page 126)

092 Baked Apples

PREPARATION TIME 10 minutes   **COOKING TIME** 35–40 minutes   **SERVES** 4

4 large dessert apples, such as Braeburn
40g/1½oz caster sugar
1 tsp ground cinnamon
50g/1¾oz marzipan, chopped
25g/1oz blanched almonds, chopped

50g/1¾oz/scant ⅓ cup dried apricots,
    chopped
knob of unsalted butter, chopped
Greek yogurt or vanilla ice cream, to serve

1 Preheat the oven to 180°C/350°F/Gas 4. Using an apple corer, remove the apple cores.
  Then, with the point of a small sharp knife, cut an incision about 2cm/¾in deep around the
  circumference of each apple. Place the apples in a greased baking dish.
2 Mix the sugar with the cinnamon, then add the marzipan, almonds and apricots and use to
  fill the centres of the apples. Add a small piece of butter to the top. Pour a little water into
  the base of the dish.
3 Bake in the preheated oven for 35–40 minutes, until the apples are tender.

093 Pears with Chocolate Sauce

PREPARATION TIME 5 minutes   COOKING TIME 8 minutes   SERVES 4

4 ripe but firm pears, quartered and cored
unsalted butter, melted, for brushing

CHOCOLATE SAUCE
75g/2½oz good-quality plain chocolate
(at least 70% cocoa solids), chopped
50g/1¾oz cocoa powder
25g/1oz caster sugar, or to taste

1 Preheat the grill to high. Brush the pears with melted butter then cook on a grill rack under the preheated grill for about 4 minutes on each side until warmed, slightly softened and lightly charred.
2 Meanwhile, make the sauce by melting the chocolate in 125ml/4fl oz/½ cup boiling water in a small bowl placed over a saucepan of hot water. Stir regularly until smooth.
3 Dissolve the cocoa powder and sugar in 2 tablespoons boiling water, then pour into the melted chocolate, stirring. Serve the pears with the warm sauce poured over.

094 **Caramel Oranges**

PREPARATION TIME 15 minutes   **COOKING TIME** 15 minutes   **SERVES** 4

4 large oranges
115g/4oz/½ cup caster sugar

vanilla ice cream, plain yogurt or crème
fraîche, to serve

1 Working over a bowl to catch any juice, carefully cut away all the orange skin and white pith. Reserve some of the skin. Cut across each orange to make about 6 slices.
2 Remove the pith from the peel, then cut the peel into very fine shreds. Blanch these in boiling water for 2–3 minutes until tender. Drain and dry.
3 Put the sugar and 75ml/2½fl oz/⅓ cup water in a small saucepan and heat gently until the sugar dissolves, stirring gently. Bring the mixture to the boil and cook until it is a light caramel colour. Pour over the oranges and set aside to chill for a few hours.
4 Scatter the orange peel over the oranges and serve with a scoop of vanilla ice cream, plain yogurt or crème fraîche.

095 Seared Pears with Cardamom Butter

PREPARATION TIME 15 minutes   **COOKING TIME** 8–12 minutes   **SERVES** 4

4 ripe but firm pears, cored and
thickly sliced
caster sugar or brown sugar,
for sprinkling

CARDAMOM BUTTER
75g/2½oz unsalted butter, diced
1½ tsp lemon juice
seeds from 3 crushed cardamom pods

1 Preheat the grill to high. Make the cardamom butter by melting the butter with the lemon juice
and cardamom seeds in a small saucepan.
2 Brush the pear slices with some of the butter and sprinkle with sugar. Cook the slices on an
oiled grill rack under the preheated grill, turning occasionally and brushing with the butter,
for 4–6 minutes on each side until softening and beginning to caramelize. Serve the pears
with any remaining butter spooned over.

096 Chocolate Brioche Sandwiches

PREPARATION TIME 10 minutes   **COOKING TIME** 5 minutes   **SERVES** 4

4 brioche rolls, split
good-quality apricot conserve,
  for spreading

150g/5½oz good-quality plain chocolate,
  grated
vanilla ice cream, to serve (optional)

1 Preheat the grill to medium. Spread each brioche roll half with a little conserve. Sprinkle the chocolate over the 4 bottom halves and cover with the top halves, pressing them together.

2 Cook on a grill rack under the preheated grill for 2–3 minutes until the top is beginning to colour. Turn carefully and press gently with a fish slice, then cook on the other side until the chocolate has melted.

3 Serve the sandwiches straightaway, either on their own or accompanied by vanilla ice cream.

097 Fudgy Bananas

PREPARATION TIME 5 minutes   **COOKING TIME** 15 minutes   **SERVES** 4

4 bananas, peeled

75g/2½oz vanilla fudge, coarsely chopped

4 tbsp rum

vanilla ice cream, to serve

1 Preheat the oven to 200°C/400°F/Gas 6. Cut a slit along the length of each banana and push some of the fudge into it. Wrap each banana in kitchen foil, sealing the edges securely.

2 Place the bananas on a baking sheet and cook in the preheated oven for 10–15 minutes, depending on the ripeness of the bananas.

3 Remove from the oven and serve with the vanilla ice cream.

098 Plums with Cinnamon Cream

PREPARATION TIME 10 minutes   **COOKING TIME** 15 minutes   **SERVES** 4

8 large, ripe but not too soft plums,
  halved and pitted
1 tbsp clear honey, warmed slightly
knob of unsalted butter, chopped

CINNAMON CREAM
225ml/8fl oz/scant 1 cup double cream
½ tsp cinnamon
1 tbsp icing sugar

1 Preheat the oven to 180°C/350°F/Gas 4.
2 Put the plum halves in an ovenproof dish, drizzle the honey over the top and dot with butter. Cover with foil and bake in the preheated oven for about 15 minutes until tender.
3 Meanwhile, make the cinnamon cream by whipping the cream to soft peaks. Mix the cinnamon with the sugar and fold into the cream.
4 Remove the plums from the oven and serve with the juices and cinnamon cream.

099 Summer Berry Parcels

PREPARATION TIME 15 minutes, plus 30 minutes infusing   **COOKING TIME** 10 minutes   **SERVES** 4

450g/1lb frozen mixed summer fruits,
  thawed
3–4 tbsp golden caster sugar
5 tbsp orange juice
1 tbsp lemon juice
2 tbsp brandy

CARDAMOM CREAM
2–3 cardamom pods, split
about 1½ tsp caster sugar, or to taste
300ml/10½fl oz/scant 1¼ cups single
  or whipping cream

1 Make the cardamom cream by heating the cardamom, sugar and cream in a heavy-based
  saucepan until it boils. Remove from the heat, cover the pan and leave to infuse for 30 minutes.
  Strain, cool completely and then chill. Preheat the oven to 180°C/350°F/Gas 4.
2 Divide the fruits among 4 squares of heavy-duty foil large enough to enclose the fruits.
3 Warm the brandy caster sugar and fruit juices in a small saucepan until the sugar has dissolved.
  Pour the syrup over the fruits.
4 Fold the foil loosely over the fruits and twist the edges together firmly to secure. Put the parcels
  on a baking tray and cook for about 10 minutes in the preheated oven until heated through.
5 Taste the cardamom cream for sweetness, sprinkle over more sugar if needed, and serve with
  the fruit parcels.

100 Queen of Puddings

PREPARATION TIME 5 minutes, plus 30 minutes soaking   **COOKING TIME** 30 minutes   **SERVES** 6

15g/½oz/1 tbsp butter, plus extra
   for greasing
570ml/20fl oz/scant 2⅓ cups milk
grated zest of ½ lemon

75g/2½oz/scant ⅓ cup caster sugar
115g/4oz/1½ cups fresh white breadcrumbs
2 eggs, separated
3 tbsp plum, blackcurrant or strawberry jam

1 Preheat the oven to 180°C/350°F/Gas 4. Butter 6 ramekin dishes and place on a baking sheet.

2 Put the milk, lemon zest and 2 tablespoons of the sugar into a heavy-based saucepan and heat gently until the sugar has dissolved, then remove from the heat and stir in the breadcrumbs and egg yolks. Pour the mixture into the dishes and leave to soak for 30 minutes.

3 Bake the puddings in the preheated oven for about 20 minutes until just set. Remove from the oven and increase the temperature to 190°C/375°F/Gas 5.

4 Warm the jam a little in a small saucepan, then carefully spread it over the top of the puddings.

5 Whisk the egg whites until they hold soft peaks. Gradually add the remaining 50g/1¾oz sugar, whisking well after each addition, until the mixture is smooth and glossy. Swirl the meringue over the puddings and bake for 8–10 minutes until golden brown.

INDEX